BIBLICAL FINANCE

REFLECTIONS ON
MONEY, WEALTH & POSSESSIONS

CROWN FINANCIAL MINISTRIES

Copyright © 2010 by Crown Financial Ministries, UK
All rights reserved

Published by Crown Financial Ministries UK

Photocopying or any other form of duplication is strictly prohibited

Typesetting and layout design by Fleur Isbell

Cover design by Christian Scott, Hillsong, London

Unless otherwise stated, Scripture quotations are taken from Holy Bible: New International Version – UK, Copyright ©
1973, 1978, 1984 by the International Bible Society.

Verses identified as NASB are taken from the New American Standard Bible, Copyright © 1960, 1962, 1963, 1968, 1971,
1972, 1973, 1975, 1977, 1995 by the Lockman Foundation.

Verses identified as NLT are taken from the Holy Bible: New Living Translation, Copyright © 1996, 2004 by Tyndale
Charitable Trust. Used by permission of Tyndale House Publishers.

Verses identified as AMP are taken from the Amplified Bible, Copyright © 1954, 1958, 1962, 1964, 1965, 1987 by the
Lockman Foundation.

Verses identified as MSG are taken from The Message, Copyright © 1993, 1994, 1995, 1996, 2000, 2001, 2002 by
Eugene H. Peterson.

Verses identified as KJV are taken from the King James Version of the Bible: Public Domain.

Verses identified as RSV are taken from Revised Standard Version, Copyright © 1973 by the Zondervan Corporation.

ISBN: 978-0-9563950-2-3

Printed in the United Kingdom

FOREWORD

This book is literally a God-send! The Bible is an immensely practical book and, as the *Biblical Finance* devotional demonstrates, has much clear common sense to give when it comes to handling money. This is a subject that causes many Christians to feel nervous – and we can feel guilty if we think we have too much and equally bad if we think we have too little!

We live in a time when many of us are suffering from the consequences of both governments and individuals not handling money as the Bible suggests. The problems of unemployment and over-indebtedness would be greatly reduced if these principles had been followed through.

Mark has written a devotional that will really help change our lives. Full of spiritual wisdom and practical insight it offers not just practical help but eternal hope as well. Covering a range of topics from priorities to integrity in handling money; from debt through giving to saving it is packed with godly wisdom. The devotional also strongly reminds us that we belong to another Kingdom and that, thanks to our beloved Jesus, the wonder of heaven stretches before us for evermore.

Not only that, but at the end there is a detailed list of all the 2,350 verses that provide guidance on all kinds of money matters. It will therefore be a really useful reference as well as a devotional that will inspire you to grow in faith.

It is a truly wonderful book and I wholly commend it to you.

Keith Tondeur, founder of Credit Action

ACKNOWLEDGEMENTS

I want to express my deepest thanks to those who have significantly influenced this devotional. They include Rev. Osien Sibanda, who undertook some of the early research. I thank my wife, Rhoda, for her wisdom and enthusiasm. I am grateful to my editors, Gillian Searl, Neil Elliott and William Womble, my Sunday School leader when I was a member at First Baptist, Woodstock, Georgia, USA. I am grateful for the valuable contribution to the content made by Tim and Jocelyn Segedin of Hillsong Church, London.

Special thanks is due to Edward Hobbs, Director of Stewardship Ministries at First Baptist, Woodstock, who kindly allowed me to use resources from some of the ministry programs he has developed while counselling those in need of godly counsel.

I am grateful to the team at Crown Financial Ministries who have sought faithfully to teach what the Bible says about our money and possessions. Some of the insights of the founders of this ministry, Larry Burkett (1939-2003) and Howard Dayton, are also included.

Over the years I have been greatly enriched by reading some of the enduring hymns and words of saints who in many instances now live in heavenly places and I have taken the opportunity of sharing some of these inspiring words. I have even recorded some words of those who may not have known Jesus Christ as Lord and Saviour, but who expressed words of wisdom that are aligned with the Bible. It is a privilege to be the author of a book that includes the words of Aiden Tozer, John Bunyan, Billy Graham, John Maxwell, Ron Blue, Epictetus, John Calvin, Martin Luther, Hudson Taylor, Randy Alcorn, Johnny Hunt and many others.

Mark Lloydbottom

Crown Financial Ministries
www.crownuk.org

AUTHOR'S INTRODUCTION

Our lives are interwoven with decisions about money and possessions. Those with enough have as many challenges as those who do not.

I was inspired to write this devotional study by Rhoda, my wife, who commits herself at the outset of each day to read her Oswald Chambers devotional. I thought that it would be valuable to record insights that provide both spiritual and, in the case of some days, practical steps about how to handle money and possessions.

Never before have there been so many opportunities to spend and the money we spend is often not ours – it is borrowed. For some, their wealth defines them. For Christians it is our faith that defines us although we recognise that we conform in so many ways to society's ways and means.

Each day's reading is accompanied by 'words of wisdom'. These are intended to be insights and reflections as you study each day.

I refer to the 2,350 verses that are in the Bible and refer throughout to what God says about how we are to handle our money and possessions. This devotional includes more than 300 verses while the appendices include references to the 2,350 verses in 20 different categories.

About Mark Lloydbottom and Crown Financial Ministries

Mark is the founder of Crown Financial Ministries in the UK. Crown operates around the world and seeks to equip people worldwide to learn, apply and teach God's financial principles so they may know Christ more intimately, be free to serve Him and help fund the Great Commission.

CONTENTS PAGE OVERVIEW

APPENDIX CONTENTS

Day

01

A BIBLICAL ANSWER

The Bible amazingly reveals God's plans. *"In the beginning was the Word, and the Word was with God, and the Word was God...and the Word became flesh and made His dwelling among us"* (John 1:1,14). Jesus the Word was there before the beginning and the role the members of the holy trinity played in Creation is made clear in Genesis. God's written Word is powerful today. It teaches us everything we need for life: *"as His divine power has given to us all things that pertain to life and godliness"* (2 Peter 1:3, NKJV) and indicates we can live to please Him (Ephesians 2:10). It even teaches us "how" to please him: for example in our social interactions, as employees, in marital and family relationships, and in the handling of money and possessions. The Living Word (Jesus Christ) gave us the written Word so that we will know the extent of what He has done for us and how to live for Him.

How amazing to know God's only Son, Jesus, died that we might live forever. God's love is so great that He prepares a place for us in eternity. Our life on earth is so short although in younger years it does not appear to be so. The Bible reminds us that we may have a life span of just over 600,000 hours (seventy five years), yet He cares for us moment by moment and day by day.

The only book God has written

The Bible is the only book that God ever wrote. The Bible is where we can look to find how much God loves us, how to live, how to avoid problems, how to fix problems, how to succeed and how to live our lives according to His Word. Unlike other handbooks, however, the Bible needs no updates. Furthermore it does not start at the beginning or finish at the

The Word of God well understood and religiously obeyed is the shortest route to spiritual perfection. And we must not select a few favourite passages to the exclusion of others. Nothing less than a whole Bible can make a whole Christian.

A W Tozer

I am profitably engaged in reading the Bible. Take all of this Book that you can by reason and the balance by faith, and you will live and die a better man.

Abraham Lincoln

> *For the word of God is living and active. Sharper than any double-edged sword, it penetrates even to dividing soul and spirit, joints and marrow; it judges the thoughts and attitudes of the heart.*
>
> **Hebrews 4:12**

- -

end with life on earth, for at the end of life on earth eternity is promised!

This 30-day devotional journey is grounded in Scripture and godly wisdom. The church in Thessalonica received the Word with readiness and searched the Scriptures to find out whether what the disciples taught was true (Acts 17:11). Since the Bible is our reference source let us look at its background – after all it is the book to which Christians turn to learn more about God, His ways, His plans, and His purposes.

> *I am a creature of a day. I am a spirit come from God, and returning to God. I want to know one thing: the way to heaven. God himself has condescended to teach me the way. He has written it down in a book. Oh, give me that book! At any price give me the book of God. Let me be a man of one book.*
>
> **John Wesley**

Bible facts

The word 'Bible' means 'books.' There are 66 of them comprising 1,189 chapters – in the King James version that includes 31,102 verses and more than 775,000 words! The Bible was written over a period of 1,500 years – the oldest book is Job, whose authorship is unknown. There were more than 40 authors whose occupations were as diverse as kings, peasants, philosophers, tentmakers, shepherds, fishermen and scholars. It was written on three continents (Asia, Africa and Europe) and in three languages (Hebrew, Aramaic and Greek). It includes more than 1,200 promises, almost 6,500 commands and over 8,000 predictions.

Although the Bible may have been penned by men the author is unquestionably God himself. In the middle chapter and verse (Psalm 118: 8) we read the Bible's central theme that it is, "*better to trust in God than in man.*"

If you want to find out what God wants you to know about prayer or faith you have a resource of about 500 Bible verses for each. If you want to learn what God has to say about how we handle our money, wealth and possessions there are 700 direct verses referring to money and in total 2,350 verses referring to money, wealth and possessions. Fifteen per cent of Jesus' recorded words are about handling money and possessions. If you have listened to a preacher and thought that the Bible spoke mainly about giving (to the church), be blessed, amazed and encouraged as you study these thirty devotional readings. The sheer scale of what the Bible has to say demands our attention for it is clear that God knows the financial temptations that lie in this area. And His wisdom found in Scripture will help you avoid many financial pitfalls.

Your daily devotions

We are living in a time of massive economic upheaval and instability. It is evident that man's economy is flawed and does not work, we need a 'God answer' to this worldly problem. This devotional journey will focus on discovering what God has to say in the area of handling money and possessions.

These daily devotions are not a replacement for your own Bible study. Devotions illuminate the truth of the Bible and give us understanding when we allow the Holy Spirit to speak to our inner self through meditation and prayer – telling God what you want Him to know and listening to Him. Prayer is indeed a two-way process of speaking *to* God and listening *for* God.

God's financial system unveiled

In 2 Timothy 3:16 we read, "*all Scripture is given by inspiration of God and is profitable for doctrine, reproof, for correction, for instruction in righteousness*" (KJV). Note that the Bible says *all* Scripture and not some. Through faith we accept Jesus Christ as Saviour. If our salvation is only about eternity why would we not go directly to heaven instead of living here on earth? It is because our purpose on earth is to share our faith and live a life that pleases Him.

There is a close correlation between our true spiritual condition and how we handle our money and possessions. There are many areas where we may wonder how God wants us to handle our finances but we do not need to conjecture because the Bible is very clear in this area. God's biblical financial system differs from that of the world's – and one of the main differences is that God's economy works whereas the world's does not! God's economy says you are more blessed by giving than receiving. God promises much for our obedience, especially in financial matters as we shall explore during these devotional studies.

He chose to give us birth through the word of truth, that we might be a kind of firstfruits of all he created.

James 1:18

Day 02

SEEKING WISDOM

Take care to get what you like, or you will be forced to like what you get.

George Bernard Shaw

It is believed that the first Bible book written was the book of Job. In Job 28: 12-13 we hear Job in his discourse asking, *"Where can wisdom be found? Where does understanding dwell? Man does not comprehend its worth."* Solomon also regarded wisdom above all and instructs his sons in Proverbs 4:7 that, *"wisdom is supreme; therefore get wisdom. Though it cost you all you have, get understanding."* But what is wisdom and how do we get it?

What is wisdom?

Wisdom is the practical use of knowledge; it is us knowing what to do with the knowledge that He gives us. It is the ability to discern God's hand in human circumstances and apply heavenly judgement to earthly situations. Wisdom is godly understanding – God's perspective given to us that allows us to take something that seems complex and make it simple. Whereas wisdom takes the complicated and simplifies it we often do the opposite – take what is simple and make it complicated! Wisdom takes our confusion and replaces it with clarity. It is a gift of heart and mind that is needed for right conduct in life. Wisdom in the Bible is always accompanied by humility and the fear of the Lord.

Looking to God

Often, when we are in the midst of situations and want answers we look within ourselves or look around at others, but the Bible encourages us that in order to get wisdom we need to look up to God. Paul tells the believers at Ephesus: *"I keep asking that the God of our Lord Jesus Christ, the glorious Father, may give you the Spirit of wisdom and revelation so that you may know Him better"* (Ephesians 1:17). James also tells us to look to God for wisdom, *"If any of* you lacks wisdom, he should ask God, who gives generously to all without finding fault, and it will be given to him" (James 1:5).

Take action

The solution to successful financial management is found in the Bible. At the end of this devotional are over 2000 Bible references which will provide you with knowledge in the area of handling money, belongings and finance. The following devotions seek to highlight some of the key areas of biblical finance and give you a practical guide to implementation. But remember, wisdom is the practical use of knowledge; to obtain tangible results, and positive changes in your finances any knowledge you gain in this book needs to be applied, to be acted on.

In Dr Henry Cloud's book *"9 Things You Simply Must Do"*, one of the chapters is entitled *"Do something."* In this chapter it says:

"He did not plan for us to sit back and allow life to follow the course of least resistance, becoming miserable, oppressive, unjust, full of mistakes, unloving, poverty stricken, ugly, lazy, negative, and evil without moving to do something about it. Such passivity is as far from reflecting the image of God as one could imagine. To the degree that we allow life just to happen and are not active forces to change whatever situation we find ourselves in, we are not living up to our true humanity by reflecting God's nature. And that may be the reason that you are stuck and not getting to where you want to be. Be who God created you to be. Get active...Get moving!"

This is the pivotal thing to understand; just reading God's word and knowing what it says is not going to get you anywhere, you must act. Good intent in the application of knowledge means little and will most likely result in little. James tells us directly, *"But don't just listen to God's word. You must do what it says. Otherwise you are only fooling yourselves"* (James 1:22). What is even harder is that to see results in our lives, we also need the discipline to act on God's word in a consistent manner for a sustained period of time. Sporadic application of knowledge is unlikely to generate change in our lives. So why not decide from the outset to make notes, highlight key verses and thoughts throughout these devotional studies, and then make plans on paper to implement and follow through. Make sure you have someone to whom you keep yourself accountable in this area, share your goals and plans with them and remember that God is there to help us if we ask."

Listen to advice and accept instruction, and in the end you will be wise.

Proverbs 19:20
- -

Day 03

COUNSEL

Yesterday we looked at the importance of seeking God's wisdom. Today we will consider what the Bible has to say about seeking counsel.

Seeking counsel

What prevents us from seeking counsel? There are two common reasons – pride and stubbornness. As for pride, our culture often perceives seeking advice as a sign of weakness. We are told, "Stand on your own two feet; you don't need anyone to help make your decisions for you." Stubbornness is characterised by positions such as, "Don't confound me with facts; my mind is already made up."

God encourages us to use a great gift He has provided for our benefit – godly counsel. In Proverbs 19:20 we read, "*listen to advice and accept instruction, and in the end you will be wise.*" While Proverbs 12:15 says, "*the way of a fool seems right to him, but a wise man listens to advice.*" And Proverbs 10:8 says, "*the wise man is glad to be instructed, but a self-sufficient fool falls flat on his face*" (TLB).

We seek counsel to gain insights, suggestions and alternatives that will assist us in making decisions from a godly perspective.

Sources of counsel

Scripture: What does the Bible have to say on a particular issue? The Psalmist wrote, "*your laws are both my light and my counsellors,*" (Psalm 119:24, TLB) and further on in Psalm 119:98-100, "*Your commands make me wiser than my enemies.... I have more insight than all my teachers, for I meditate on your statutes.... I have more understanding than the* *elders, for I obey your precepts."* Proverbs tells us why counsel is so important because, *"plans fail for lack of counsel"* (15:22).

> *Expect great things from God; attempt great things for God!"*
> **William Carey,**
> **English Baptist missionary, 1761-1834**

The Bible makes this remarkable claim about itself: *"for the word of God is living and active. Sharper than any double-edged sword...it judges the thoughts and attitudes of the heart"* (Hebrews 4:12). The truths in the Bible are enduring and timeless. If the Bible provides clear direction regarding a financial matter we have within us the knowledge to follow God's Word. If the Bible is not specific about an issue, we should subject our decision to the second source of counsel:

Plans fail for lack of counsel, but with many advisers they succeed.

Proverbs 15:22

The counsel of godly people

"The mouth of the righteous man utters wisdom, and his tongue speaks what is just. The law of his God is in his heart; his feet do not slip" (Psalm 37:30-31). The Christian life is not one of independence from other Christians but of interdependence on one another. God has given each of us certain abilities and gifts, but He has not given any one person all the abilities that he or she needs to be most productive.

Your spouse
If you are married, the first person you need to consult is your spouse, and in so doing you should enhance your relationship. Be sure to avoid the trap of allowing a situation to become a source of strife and friction. Consulting your spouse also honours him or her and, when it comes to finances, helps each spouse plan and prepare for times ahead.

Your parents
If you are not married, parents are an important source of counsel. They have years of experience and they know you well.

One of the surest ways to succeed at something is to spend time with a person who has done just that.

Phil Pringle, Church planter, Sydney

Church leaders
Those to whom we look for spiritual guidance and direction.

Experienced people
If they are not Christian you may wish to share their counsel with those who are.

A multitude of counsellors
Ecclesiastes 4:8-12 tells us that two are better than one.

The counsel of the Lord
At all times it is important to refer back to the Lord the counsel you receive. After all, one of His names is Wonderful Counsellor.

Counsel to avoid
Avoid the counsel of the wicked. My definition of wicked for these purposes is, "one who lives in a manner that disregards or is against God."

These include fortune tellers, mediums, spiritualists and horoscopes.

Earthly goods are given to be used, not to be collected. Hoarding is idolatry.

Dietrich Bonhoeffer

Avoid biased counsel – that which is not impartial or independent. When receiving financial advice, ask yourself these questions: "What stake does this person have in the outcome of my decisions? How does he or she stand to gain or lose from this decision?" If the adviser will profit, be cautious when evaluating his or her advice and always seek a second, unbiased opinion.

And finally...
When you are making a decision it may be helpful to withdraw to a quiet place where you can draw on the resources from heaven – your faith, the Bible, and prayer.

Day 04

GOD'S PART AND OUR PART

Gold is a symbol of value and a rare mineral. For centuries many cultures, including western countries, have regarded it as a safe investment. It is estimated that there are only five billion ounces of gold on this earth. How much is that? Imagine a 20-metre cube (you could have two such cubes in one half of a football pitch) – that is all the space you need to store all the gold in the world! Five billion ounces, much of it locked away stored in bank vaults. Who owns all this gold? Who is the true owner?

God owns it all

In 1 Chronicles 29:11-12 we read that, "*everything in the heavens and earth is yours, O Lord and this is your Kingdom. We adore you as being in control of everything*" (TLB). Psalm 24:1, Deuteronomy 10:14 and Paul in 1 Corinthians 10:26 all attest to the fact, "*that the earth is the Lord's and everything in it.*" Leviticus 25:23 and Psalm 50:10-12 tell us just some of what God owns – "*the land, the cattle, the birds,*" while Paul writes in 1 Corinthians 6:20, "*we too have been bought for a price...therefore glorify God in your body, and in your spirit, which are God's*" (NKJV). And Haggai 2:8 makes it clear that God owns all the gold. In Tutankhamen's day it was believed that when you died you could take your possessions with you, but the seventh verse and sixth chapter of the first letter of Timothy says, "*it is certain we can carry nothing out*" (1 Timothy 6:7, NKJV); Paul makes it clear no balances are transferred to us anywhere after we die.

The world asks: "What does a person own?" God asks, "How is the person using what they have been given?" Your use of money shows what you think of God. We will be judged on the basis of our loyalty to Christ with the time, talents, and treasures that were at our disposal.

Erwin W. Lutzer, Pastor, Moody church

Recognising God's ownership

Acknowledging God's ownership requires a transformation of the way we think – and that takes time as the revelation from God's Word sends spiritual pulses from the brain to the heart. Recognising God's ownership is an essential component of becoming content. When you believe you own a particular possession, the circumstances surrounding it will affect your attitude.

God is our provider

As Matthew states, the Lord promises to provide our needs: *"Seek first his Kingdom and his righteousness, and all these things will be given to you as well"* (6:33). To what extent does He provide? One of the ways we can understand God better is to look at His names as these always reveal an aspect or attribute of His character. In Genesis 22, Abraham revealed a new name for God; Jehovah-Jireh which can be translated "God will provide" or "God sees." Ours is a God who sees our need before it arises and makes provision for it. Do you know him as this kind of God?"

Our part

Recognising that we are stewards means that we must manage what He owns. God has given us the responsibility of being stewards, *"you made him ruler over the works of your hands; you put everything under his feet"* (Psalm 8:6). We are called to be faithful stewards with all that we are given, as illustrated by the parable of the talents in Matthew 25:14-15. God requires us to be faithful with all our money, wealth and possessions.

Being faithful

We are charged to be faithful in handling 100 per cent of our income, not just 10 per cent. We have allowed ourselves to learn how to handle the 90 per cent from the world's perspective and not from God's.

In the parable of the unjust manager (Luke 16:1-2) we read, *"There was a rich man whose manager* [steward] *was accused of wasting his possessions. So he called him in and asked, 'What is this I hear about you? Give an account of your management, because you cannot be manager* [steward] *any longer."'*

This passage teaches two principles. First, when we waste or mismanage our possessions it could become public knowledge and create a poor testimony. Second, God may remove us as stewards if we squander what He has given to us.

As we are faithful in little things, then God knows He can trust us with greater responsibilities. Small things are small things, but faithfulness with a small thing is a big thing.

Development of character

God uses money to refine our character. As David McConaughy explained in his book, Money the Acid Test (written in 1918), "*Money, most common of temporal things, involves uncommon and eternal consequences. Even though it may be done quite unconsciously, money moulds people in the process of getting it, saving it, spending it, and giving it. Depending on how it's used, it proves to be a blessing or a curse. Either the person becomes master of the money, or the money becomes the master of the person. Our Lord uses money to test our lives and as an instrument to mould us into the likeness of himself.*"

This book of the law shall not depart out of thy mouth; but thou shalt meditate therein day and night, that thou mayest observe to do according to all that is written therein: for then thou shalt make thy way prosperous, and then thou shalt have good success

Joshua 1:8, KJV

- -

Day 05

THE CHARACTER OF STEWARDSHIP

The story is told of a man who went to John Wesley to report that his house was on fire. "*Mr. Wesley...your house has burned to the ground,*" he said, to which Wesley replied, "*No. The Lord's house burned to the ground. That means one less responsibility for me.*" John Wesley understood the principle of stewardship – we are privileged to be stewards of what God owns, and He owns all things.

'Steward' can be defined as: *Someone entrusted with another's wealth or property and charged with the responsibility of managing it in the owner's best interest – not ours.*

Job understood the principle well. After he lost his family and property he understood that he did not own anything and refused to blame or curse God. Understanding stewardship alleviates stress and allows God to take charge.

We are managers

Stewardship recognises that, "*God owns everything and I am His manager/steward.*" Almost every book in the Bible refers to the Genesis account of creation. He created everything and what He asks of us is to live without allowing wealth or possessions to become the focus of our attention. He is a jealous God and He knows us from the beginning to the end of our days. He knows our weaknesses and frailties, and He knows that unless we submit what we have to Him we will not have an eternal perspective. He wants us to be good managers until we go to be with Him or the Lord's return – whichever comes first.

The earth is the Lord's, and everything in it, the world, and all who live in it.

Psalm 24:1

Some may find the subject of stewardship particularly difficult in two main areas: children, wealth and possessions. The earth is the Lord's and everything in it and even those who dwell in it. Understanding true ownership is an important element in managing what we have. It helps us to obey the Word when instructed to give and help the poor or destitute. It becomes a privilege to help the needy around us as we see God's provision not only for ourselves but also for others.

God delegates to us the authority over His Creation and commands us to manage and look after it all (Genesis 1:28). This refers not just to animals, ourselves, our family or our possessions but to everything over which we have influence. God requires us to be responsible and good managers of whatever He has given us, and in this respect we are working for God. There is a judgement coming and we are required to use God's resources wisely.

The heaven, even the heavens, are the Lord's: but the earth hath he given to the children of men.
Psalm 115:16, KJV

We are to be faithful and accountable

Two characteristics stand out when we recognise this perspective of stewardship. The first is the faithfulness to the owner and the second is accountability because the owner can come at anytime and do some stocktaking. In the parable of the talents (Matthew 25:14-30) we learn that a servant is required to be faithful. We must be faithful with what God entrusts to us. He promised that He would reward us for using his assets wisely. The more we have, the more assiduous we should be in using wisely what the master has put in our hands. Stewards are not to be lazy; they should be wise, seeking opportunities for growth and increase. The master is coming and he will deal with us according to how we have used our talents, possessions, influence and our lives. This parable teaches us that all those who are unproductive will lose what they are given.

A faithful man will be richly blessed, but one eager to get rich will not go unpunished.
Proverbs 28:20

The steward's life is to please and obey the master's instructions – and the Bible is replete with principles, instructions and wisdom. A wise steward uses what has been entrusted to them for God's glory and the building of His Kingdom. Unwise stewards use people and possessions selfishly.

Stewardship is the acceptance from God of personal responsibility for all of life and life's affairs.

Roswell C Long

How much can God trust you with?

Whoever can be trusted with very little can also be trusted with much, and whoever is dishonest with very little will also be dishonest with much. So if you have not been trustworthy in handling worldly wealth, who will trust you with true riches? And if you have not been trustworthy with someone else's property, who will give you property of your own? No servant can serve two masters. Either he will hate the one and love the other, or he will be devoted to the one and despise the other.

Luke 16:10-13

Your bank and credit card are theological. They tell you who and what you worship.

No compromise

"You cannot serve both God and money. The Pharisees, who loved money, heard all this and were sneering at Jesus. He said to them, 'You are the ones who justify yourselves in the eyes of men, but God knows your hearts. What is highly valued among men is detestable in God's sight.'"

Luke 16:13-15

Day 06

WHAT IS OUR ATTITUDE TOWARD OUR TREASURES?

What captivates your mind? What do you think about? What do you treasure? What do you spend doing longer than you perhaps ought to? What do you spend your money on?

Shopping has become a national obsession – the traffic queue outside our church heading for the shopping centre at one o'clock on a Sunday afternoon suggests that the traditional family Sunday lunch is not the national appointment it used to be.

How many hours do you spend each week looking at a screen, whether a TV, game machine, mobile phone or a computer? Whatever the heart pursues dominion will ensue. If we pursue fleshly pursuits we will care less for the things of the Spirit but if we pursue the things of the Spirit we will concern ourselves less with the flesh. But ever since the fall of man in the Garden of Eden there has been an ongoing battle between flesh and spirit. Where the pursuit of riches holds dominion in the heart, God has lost His authority within.

Christians cannot experience peace in the area of their finances until they have surrendered total control of this area to God and accepted their position as stewards.

Larry Burkett

Where is your treasure?

Matthew tells us, *"for where your treasure is, there your heart will be also"* (6:21, NKJV). Here Jesus is telling us that our heart (desires, hopes, wants) is closely tied to our treasure. In fact, your heart often follows your money. If Jesus alerts us to this powerful tug of our heart it must be something we should pay close attention to. If you want to find out where your treasure is then examine your bank and credit card statements and you will see which side of this tug-of-war is winning. Your priorities will be evident from these statements. The spending of your income indicates where your heart is.

Don't waste your God-given life with low living, small planning, mundane talking, constant grumbling, or cheap giving. Be all God called you and equipped you to be.

What's your attitude?

C. S. Lewis once said, "He who has God and everything has no more than he who has God." The word 'everything' is a big word when it applies to mankind, but it diminishes greatly when mankind applies it to God.

There is a powerful correlation between a person's true spiritual condition and his or her attitude and actions concerning money and possessions. Jesus linked money and salvation together in Luke 19:9 when Zacchaeus said he would give money back to the poor and pay back four times over to anyone he had cheated. Contrast that with the rich young ruler who had kept God's commandments but when he asked Jesus how he might inherit eternal life. Jesus replied, "*Go sell your possessions and give to the poor, then come, follow me*" (Matthew 19:21). Jesus knew that wealth owned this man rather than the other way round. He said it was easier for a camel to get down on its belly and try to crawl through a very small opening than it was for a rich man to give up all his riches and enter the Kingdom of God. That same challenge is just as difficult today as it was when Jesus spoke these words.

A test of character

It has been said that how we handle money is a litmus test of our true character. It is also an index of our true spirituality.

If you are on the escalator to heaven you should not be conformed to the ways of this world – no matter how hard the path. The reality is that conformity is as natural as swimming downstream. Have you ever tried to swim against the current? It is hard and sometimes you even lose ground.

Where does a person go to get proper instruction? Well, books, magazines and the Internet are filled with advice and various plans on how to make, spend, save and invest money. How blessed we are to have the Bible from where we learn the perfect plan from the Lord Jesus Christ. Jeremiah 29:11 says, "*I know the plans I have for you,*" declares the Lord; "*plans to prosper you and not harm you, plans to give you hope and a future.*" Jesus said, "*Store up for yourselves treasures in heaven, where moth and rust does not corrupt and thieves do not steal*" (Matthew 6:20).

Yet indeed I also count all things loss for the excellence of the knowledge of Christ Jesus my Lord, for whom I have suffered the loss of all things, and count them as rubbish, that I may gain Christ.

Philippians 3:8, NKJ

- -

Where God guides He provides. What God orders, He pays for. God's work, done in God's ways, never lacks supply.

- -

Martin Luther stated, *"each of us must have the conversion of the heart and mind and purse."* Let us assume that you have had the conversion of the heart. Now we must take on a new attitude by changing our minds to match that of Christ.

What do we value most? What would we most hate to lose? What do our thoughts turn to most frequently when we are free to think of what we will? And finally, what affords us the greatest pleasure?
A W Tozer

The world will never be won to Christ with what people can conveniently spare.

Bernard Edinger

Day 07

GIVING MATERIALISM A WIDE BERTH

Blessed are they that hunger and thirst after righteousness: for they shall be filled.

Matthew 5:6, NKJV

It may help to give a definition of materialism: materialism is, 'having an undue regard for material and worldly things rather than spiritual matters. This is characterised by a preoccupation with material rather than intellectual or spiritual things.' So, based on this definition do you regard yourself as materialistic?

How materialistic are you?

You might be materialistic if you spend money you do not have or buy goods you do not really need so as to indulge yourself or to impress others. Or maybe you compare the things you do not have with the possessions of others?

Read Ecclesiastes 5:10-14 *"Whoever loves money never has money enough..."* Scripture tells us that if we look for love and fulfilment in our financial status we will never be satisfied. In the right context, material possessions can bring us joy, but when we attach greater importance to them than to things that should be more important, it harms our relationship with God and others. If we sacrifice our family or our relationship with God to have certain possessions, we are materialistic. Scripture indicates a person who is greedy for more things is an idolater (Ephesians 5:5).

One master only?

In Matthew 6:24, Jesus tells us that we cannot serve two masters. When our passion for the possessions that God allows us to have exceeds our passion for the God who gave us those possessions, we know that we are materialistic. There is nothing wrong with owning things, the problem comes when those things get in the way of our relationship with God or prevent us from accomplishing God's will in our lives.

What is greed?

Greed is the eager or selfish desire for something. When our desire for possessions consumes us and overtakes us to the point that we are not satisfied with what we have, it becomes greed. Luke 12:15 warns us to, *"Watch out! Be on your guard against all kinds of greed; a man's life does not consist in the abundance of his possessions."* Paul tells us to, *"Put to death, therefore, whatever belongs to your earthly nature... and greed, which is idolatry"* (Colossians 3:5). Greed may help us accumulate a lot of possessions but greed or possessions will not make us happy. Greed is also an offence against God and we should *"put it to death."*

Desires for a material possession usually fades once the newness wears off. Look in your garage, loft or storage room and see some of the things that you once thought were essential to life and happiness that are now not working, collecting dust, or simply adding to the general clutter. Look at the array of possessions that people seek to sell at car boot sales.

Riches

Riches can be defined as an abundance of whatever is precious. Looked at in this perspective whether a person is rich or not depends on what we consider precious. What do you regard as precious?

> *All that truly matters is what we can do for the Kingdom of God. The things we accumulate are not important; they are only tools for us to use in accomplishing God's work. God owns it all anyway. The accumulation of money is a major deterrent to a humble spirit. The tendency is to desire to be served rather than to serve.*
> **Larry Burkett, Co Founder, Crown Financial Ministries, 1939-2003**

Some people want to make as much as they can, put the lid on the can and then sit on the can.

More than £6,000 is spent annually on marketing for every person in the country.

Where riches hold the dominion of the heart, God has lost dominion of the heart, God has lost His authority.

John Calvin

Your relationship with God

Paul says, *"What is more, I consider everything a loss compared to the surpassing greatness of knowing Christ Jesus my Lord, for whose sake I have lost all things. I consider them rubbish, that I may gain Christ"* (Philippians 3:7-8). Paul tapped into God's riches and realised that what the world had to offer was not even close to what God had given him. We have received a "precious faith" and "precious promises" in God's Word (2 Peter 1:1, 4). Is your faith more precious than you possessions? Is living by His precious promises valuable to you?

Then he [Jesus] said to them, "Watch out! Be on your guard against all kinds of greed; a man's life does not consist in the abundance of his possessions."

Luke 12:15

Your family

We know that we are in trouble when our financial health becomes more important than our relationship with our family. We know that we have a wrong balance in life when we spend more hours working, watching TV or 'being on the computer' than spending time building family relationships and investing our lives in them.

We might think that if we work hard we can have more money to buy more possessions for our family, but in truth instead of having larger homes and newer cars, what they really want is for us to spend more time with them. Talk to someone who is retired and I am sure they will not say they wished they had spent more time working. No. They usually say, "I wish I had spent more time with my family or growing in my relationship with God."

Eternal riches

When Jesus was about to leave this earth and ascend to Heaven, he spoke the following words to his disciples, *"In My Father's house are many mansions; if it were not so, I would have told you. I go to prepare a place for you. And if I go and prepare a place for you, I will come again and receive you to Myself; that where I am, there you may be also"* (John 14:2-3, NKJV). Jesus ascended into Heaven almost 2,000 years ago and since then He has been preparing a place for those who know Him as Lord and Saviour.

Day 08

BEING CONTENT

The so-called 'credit crunch' in 2007 was followed by increased household costs for food and energy and for a while, interest costs also increased. Unsecured debt had increased dramatically over the previous five years and many household budgets were stretched. For many, their spending was considerably greater than their income.

If we are not to fall into the trap of being a 'slave to the lender,' we must give serious consideration to planning what we spend, not extending secured borrowing to the limit, and reducing any unsecured debt.

Spend less than you earn and do it for a long time and you will be financially successful.
Ron Blue,
Kingdom Advisors

Start making a plan

Whatever your income and expenditure, having a financial plan should be a priority. Self-control starts with developing a realistic and balanced income and expenditure plan that you can use to introduce discipline into your spending – especially where you might be tempted to spend beyond your means. Creating a plan is the first important step to getting control of your finances. If you have 'no problem' with your monthly finances maybe you could look at your giving, or even at how you might reduce your outgoings. If you are having difficulty make sure you are not heading towards the day when the threatening letter arrives!

It is important to take time to record and analyse your income and expenditure, being sure to record all payments whether through your bank account, card accounts or cash.

Next make a list of everything you owe – is there anything overdue?

Finally, look at the number of cards in your wallet or purse. If any of them has money outstanding for more than two months the card is not serving you, you are serving the card company – and probably paying them at least 18 per cent interest!

You should complete the remaining daily studies before finalising your spending plan. Meanwhile, take some time to study your expenditure patterns and think about what you can reduce or eliminate. Pray through how you handle your finances and, like the widow and her plea to the prophet, call out to God and ask Him for his wisdom and help.

Learning to be content

The apostle Paul wrote in 1 Timothy 6:8, "*if we have food and covering* [clothes and shelter], *we will be content with that.*" But, our consumer-society does not want us to be content. Are there elements of your spending where you are conformed to the ways of this world? For example, a mobile phone is now deemed an absolute necessity and yet the monthly cost can easily be £30 or more; and cable television with its hundreds of channels is regarded as a household essential in many homes. Again, Paul wrote in Philippians 4:11-13, "*I have learned to be content whatever the circumstances. I know what it is to be in need and I know what it is to have plenty. I have learned the secret of being content in any and every situation, whether well fed or hungry, whether living in plenty or in want.*"

Paul learned to be content. He was not born with this instinct and neither are we; we must intentionally develop it.

Avoid coveting

Coveting means craving someone else's property, and Scripture prohibits it. The last of the Ten Commandments tells us, "*You shall not covet your neighbour's house. You shall not covert your neighbour's wife, or his manservant or maidservant,*" *his ox or donkey, or anything that belongs to your neighbour."* We could paraphrase this commandment to read: *"Do not allow your eyes and mind to stray to other women or men, or to anyone who is married; and do not desire to have a car or house like theirs, the technology they have, or holidays like they take."*

We should not use comparison to justify spending more than we should. Many people have suffered financially because they insisted on 'keeping up with the Joneses' even though they could not afford to. Someone once said, "You can never keep up with the Joneses'. Just when you thought you'd caught up, they go deeper into debt to buy more stuff!"

God can have our money and not have our hearts, but he cannot have our hearts without having our money.

R Kent Hughes

Day 09

THE TITHE

The purpose of tithing is to secure not the tithe but the tither, not the gift but the giver, not the possession but the possessor, not your money but you for God.

For some, tithing is an old fashioned religious sounding word, that can be easily dismissed as Old Testament teaching; something that isn't particularly relevant to those of us who live under grace. However it is so much more than just a word or an instruction, as it has the ability to release the blessing of God in our lives. It is a principal that existed and was practiced *before* the law and *continues* under the new covenant.

> *Honour the Lord with your capital and sufficiency* [from righteous labours] *and with the first fruits of all your income; So shall your storage places be filled with plenty, and your vats shall be overflowing with new wine.*
> **Proverbs 3:9-10, AMP**

Original sin

In order to understand tithing, we must go right back to the beginning, to when there was perfect connection between God and man. We were created by God not to live in our own efforts but to be sustained by Him. He provided Adam and Eve with a garden full of trees that were good for food, and told them; "*You are free to eat from any tree in the garden; but you must not eat from the tree of the knowledge of good and evil, for when you eat it you will surely die*" (Genesis 2:16-17)

We all know the story however; Eve and Adam ate the fruit that God told them to avoid and everything changed. God found them hiding in the garden and spoke this to them. "*Since you listened to your wife and ate from the tree whose fruit I commanded you not to eat, the ground is cursed because of you. All*

You must present as the Lord's portion the best and holiest part of everything given to you.

Numbers 18:29

your life you will struggle to scratch a living from it. It will grow thorns and thistles for you, though you will eat of its grains. By the sweat of your brow will you have food to eat until you return to the ground from which you were made. For you were made from dust, and to dust you will return" (Genesis 3:17-19, NLT).

So Adam and Eve and the rest of humanity became disconnected from God. God stepped back and left us to work things out for ourselves. However, because God created us to be sustained by him, living in relationship with him and knowing only good – we don't have the cognitive or physical capacity to live the awesome lives that God intended for us. Thus our thoughts and efforts often result in futility.

So this I say...that you must no longer live as the heathen [the Gentiles] *do in their perverseness [in the folly, vanity, and emptiness of their souls and the futility] of their minds....*[They are] *alienated* [estranged, self-banished] *from the life of God* [with no share in it; this is] *because of the ignorance* [the want of knowledge and perception, the willful blindness] *that is* deep-seated *in them, due to their hardness of heart* [to the insensitiveness of their moral nature].
Ephesians 4:17-18, AMP

Not only were we subjected to this futility but so was the rest of creation. When God created Adam he was given dominion over all the earth. When he became disconnected from God, the ground became affected; it too was cursed and subjected to the same futility that man was subjected to.

Romans 8:20-21 in the amplified Bible says: "*For the creation* [nature] *was subjected to frailty* [to futility, condemned to frustration], *not because of some intentional fault on its part, but by the will of Him Who so subjected it* [yet] *with the hope that nature* [creation] *itself will be set free from its bondage to decay and corruption* [and gain an entrance] *into the glorious freedom of God's children.*" Why is nature subjected to this futility? Why will all our efforts to be in vain, to no avail and without success no matter how hard we work? Because God created us to be sustained by Him and it has been His plan since the day of disconnect to reconnect with us. If everything we touched turned to gold, if our own efforts were

If the part of the dough offered as firstfruits is holy, then the whole batch is holy; if the root is holy, so are the branches.
Romans 11:16

- -

There are three conversions necessary: the conversion of the heart, mind, and the purse.
Martin Luther

- -

And my God will liberally supply [fill to the full] your every need according to His riches in glory in Christ Jesus. To our God and Father be glory forever and ever [through the endless eternities of the eternities].
Amen [so be it].

Philippians 4:19-20, AMP

----

successful, we wouldn't need God. So God's plan is to get us to a place where we realise that we need Him.

Jesus redeems us from death

Jesus came to earth to put right mans' curse of death that was brought about by Adam, once and for all. Jesus' death on the cross paid the price for all sin, redeemed us from death and reconciled us to God. So now, through our faith in Jesus we are considered holy and free from condemnation. Because Jesus, God's firstborn son is right with God, so we are right with God. He has reconnected us to God so that we can once again live abundant lives, sustained by Him, rather than in the futility of our own thinking. This life is not just for a chosen few, but for everyone – we simply have to take hold, by faith of what Jesus has done for us. Paul in Romans tells us, *"Here it is in a nutshell: Just as one person did it wrong and got us in all this trouble with sin and death, another person did it right and got us out of it. But more than just getting us out of trouble, he got us into life! One man said no to God and put many people in the wrong; one man said yes to God and put many in the right"* (Romans 5:18-19, MSG).

Tithing redeems our labour from futility

I never would have been able to tithe the first million I ever made if I had not tithed on my first salary, which was about $1.50 a week.

J D Rockefeller

Just as we are freed from the curse of death and made right with God through Jesus, the firstborn, we can apply the same principle when it comes to our finances. When Adam disobeyed God, the earth, our supply, the work or toil of our hands was cursed. Our supply however can be redeemed from this curse by tithing, by offering to God the first part of all our increase. The word tithe simply means a tenth and it is repeatedly stated in the Old Testament that God considers this first portion of our increase to be His. When Jesus, the Firstborn was sacrificed and given back to God, the rest of humanity was given the chance to put their faith in him and be freed from the curse of death. So it is with tithing; by returning to God what is His, we release our financial supply from its curse and give God the opportunity to pour out His blessing upon the works of our hands. By giving God His portion, the remaining 90% becomes blessed.

A tithe of everything from the land, whether grain from the soil or fruit from the trees, belongs to the Lord; it is holy to the Lord.

Leviticus 27:30

More than just money

Tithing is about more than just money; it's about putting God first, reaping His promise and living in His supply instead of trying to live under our own strength. By acting in faith, and bringing the first ten per cent of our increase back to God, we are saying, "I know that I am in your hands God and don't want to live without you at the centre of what I do." By tithing we are acknowledging that God is our supplier and reminding ourselves of what He has done for us instead of focusing on what we might try and do for Him. If we can put our trust in God in the area of our finances and learn to be confident in His supply, how much easier will it be to trust in God's provision in all areas of our lives?

Money is a terrible master but an excellent servant.

P T Barnum

Day 10

BLESSED TO BE A BLESSING

Give, and it will be given to you. A good measure, pressed down, shaken together and running over, will be poured into your lap. For with the measure you use, it will be measured to you.

Luke 6:38

He is no fool who gives what he cannot keep to gain what he cannot lose.

Jim Elliot

So when we give the first ten per cent of our income, God promises to bless us. Yet there are many verses in the Bible warning against greed and the love of money, cautioning us about the pitfalls of riches. So why then is God just waiting to pour out His blessing on us when we acknowledge his lordship with our tithe?

Our God is a God of abundance

God's intention isn't for people to live in poverty; poverty is the result of the curse. God's intention is for us to be blessed, but He wants us to be blessed through Him, not through our own endeavours. We just need to look at the Bible to see that God is not the God of shortage, or lack; He is the God of surplus, of abundance. Look at the array of creation in Genesis; it doesn't speak of stinginess but rather of an expansive God. Abraham, Isaac and Jacob all walked in relationship with God and were blessed with abundant material wealth. Even when the Israelites were made to walk in the desert because they had not trusted God, still He provided abundantly for them. Jesus' birth was celebrated with gifts of gold, incense and myrrh. When Jesus fed the 5000 there wasn't just enough, there were basketfuls left over. These stories all reveal a God of plenty not a God of scarcity, God is not stingy but has repeatedly promised to supply us with all we need; we just need to rely on Him and not on ourselves. Just look at some of these verses:

Let those who favour my righteous cause and have pleasure in my uprightness shout for joy

and be glad and say continually, Let the Lord be magnified, who takes pleasure in the prosperity of His servant.
Psalm 35:27, AMP

Bring the whole tithe into the storehouse, that there may be food in my house. Test me in this," says the Lord Almighty, "and see if I will not throw open the floodgates of heaven and pour out so much blessing that you will not have room enough for it.
Malachi 3:10

For the Lord your God will bless you as He has promised, and you will lend to many nations but will borrow from none. You will rule over many nations but none will rule over you.
Deuteronomy 15:6

Praise the Lord! How joyful are those who fear the Lord and delight in obeying his commands. Their children will be successful everywhere; an entire generation of godly people will be blessed. They themselves will be wealthy, and their good deeds will last forever. Light shines in the darkness for the godly. They are generous, compassionate, and righteous. Good comes to those who lend money generously and conduct their business fairly.
Psalm 112:1-5, NLT

Make sure you don't take things for granted and go slack in working for the common good; share what you have with others. God takes particular pleasure in acts of worship – a different kind of "sacrifice" – that take place in kitchen and workplace and on the streets.
Hebrews 13:16, MSG

Blessed to be a blessing

However, we are not blessed so that we can hold onto wealth and live an easy life; instead it is God's plan for His blessing to flow through our lives to touch other people. His blessing is not meant to be for us alone; we are blessed to be a blessing, blessed so that we can help to fulfil the heart of God. The only way that we can help others is through the prosperity of our own lives; we cannot help people out of poverty when we have nothing.

We are to use what God gives us to bless others, both in and outside the church. By living honest, open lives with others we gain a chance to express the generosity of God to them with the ultimate purpose of bringing people into relationship with God. But we need to be generous with more than just

Those who use their money totally for self-satisfaction or hoard it for that elusive "rainy day" are just as financially bound in God's eyes as those in debt. A Christian cannot be within God's will and hoard money. Those who hoard try to rationalise their behaviour with arguments that contradict God's Word.
Larry Burkett

The poorest man in the world is the man who has nothing but money.

----

our money; it's about living lives that demonstrate our understanding of all that God has done and continues to do for us. Imagine being able to reveal to others the absolute freedom, fullness and joy of a life lived under God's supply in every way; not bound by judgement and condemnation and free from financial stress and worry. This is the type of life that will be captivating to those who don't yet know God; this is the life that will cause others to want to know more about the God we serve. We are beneficiaries of what God does for us, so that others can be beneficiaries of what God does within us.

I decided that I was going to do something about this and not just turn away from the horrendous conditions of these children. If I could make a difference in the life of 'one' of these kids, if I could keep 'one' child from drinking the dog's milk, prevent 'one' child's death due to starvation and malnutrition, I would do it! Now the excitement of the possibilities and the avenues available to change the destiny of people thrills my every moment!
Biju Thampy Founder, Vision Rescue

Day 11

GENEROSITY

As Christians we need to be living under God's abundant blessing so that we can give generously to each other and to others to show the world that God provides; that He is the answer.

When we tithe, God will cause the works of our hand to flourish so that we always have enough not just for ourselves, but so that we can always be generous to others. The tithe belongs to God, but we are also called to make free will offerings above and beyond the tithe, we are commanded to be generous to others.

You're never more like Jesus than when you're giving.

**Pastor Johnny Hunt,
First Baptist, Woodstock,
Atlanta, USA**

Sowing and reaping
The Bible calls this principal sowing and reaping and God promises that He will always supply seed to those who sow generously. He will always give us more if we are faithful with what we have already been given. This principle is to encourage us in our giving; it brings a freedom and a confidence to our generosity. The principle of sowing and reaping is explained clearly in 2 Corinthians 9:6-11, *"Remember this: Whoever sows sparingly will also reap sparingly, and whoever sows generously will also reap generously. Each man should give what he has decided in his heart to give, not reluctantly or under compulsion, for God loves a cheerful giver. And God is able to make all grace abound to you, so that in all things at all times; having all that you need, you will abound in every good work. As it is written: "He has scattered abroad his gifts to the poor; his righteousness endures forever." Now he who supplies seed to the sower and bread for food will also supply and increase your store of seed and will enlarge the harvest of your righteousness. You will be made rich*

in every way so that you can be generous on every occasion, and through us your generosity will result in thanksgiving to God."

These verses show us that if we give little, we should expect little in return. If we give bountifully though, God will bless us so that we can give even more. The only way we will be able to be greater givers in the future is to begin giving generously now. Our motivation shouldn't be to give so that we can gain, it should be to give so that we can give more. We should strive to be like God who is the greatest giver of all.

Expressing God's character

Good will come to him who is generous and lends freely, who conducts his affairs with justice.

Psalm 112:5

Our God is a generous God who sent His only Son as a sacrifice for us. Jesus gave up everything, His deity, His power and eventually His life for us. Why? So that we might become rich (2 Corinthians 8:9). We who believe in Him have inherited great riches: forgiveness, adoption, justification, the indwelling of the Holy Spirit, peace with God, access to God, sanctification and eternal glory to come. As Christ's disciples we should desire to be more like Him and one way that we can do this is to give more. God gave 100 per cent, should we be happy with just 10 per cent?

God wants us to be generous like Him, not only because this type of life helps other people but because it makes our lives better too. God's word tells us that generosity brings refreshing and enlargement to our lives. Proverbs 11:24-25 puts it this way; "*One man gives freely, yet gains even more; another withholds unduly, but comes to poverty. A generous man will prosper; he who refreshes others will himself be refreshed.*"

Being generous is living unselfishly, with concern for the well being of others, free from a smallness of character or mind. This type of attitude is in direct opposition to our fallen human nature which is driven by self interest and causes us to be miserly or jealous and hoard our wealth. Therefore with every generous act, we are suppressing our old nature and giving God's nature within us a chance to express itself. By living generously we convey God's character to the world that we live in.

If a pauper gives to God, he'll feel like a prince. If a prince doesn't give to God, he'll feel like a pauper.

Plan to be generous

How long do you spend planning what you intend to give away? Does it even come close to the amount of time you spend planning what we can buy? Giving is an act that few acquire naturally, but it is at the heart of God's purpose for us. Intense competition for our resources competes with the desire to give. Perhaps we do not give because time denies us the opportunity to plan what to give away, or perhaps a deep-rooted belief that 'what is mine is mine' prevents us. What emotions do you experience when you are asked to give – unspeakable joy or feeling put on the spot?

I saw a survey in USA Today that asked people on an average income of $50,000 how much they thought they needed to be comfortable and enjoy their desired standard of living. The answer was $75,000. The same question was then asked of people with an income of $100,000 and their answer was $250,000! In other words, the more we have, the more we want.

In some respects money is like seawater – the more you drink the thirstier you get. God's way of breaking the cycle of greed is giving and it is always easier to give if we have a plan in place to do so. We have so many opportunities to give, and as one of the richer nations on this earth – an island of plenty surrounded by a world of need – we should give generously.

The wicked borrow and do not repay, but the righteous give generously.

Psalm 37:21

A generous man will himself be blessed, for he shares his food with the poor.

Proverbs 22:9

Day 12

TO WHOM DO WE GIVE?

All they asked was that we should continue to remember the poor, the very thing I was eager to do.

Galatians 2:10

Following the example of Christ we are called to be generous. We are not to just tithe but also to give generously to others. Who then are to be the recipients of our tithes and our generosity?

To the church

Our tithe must be given back to God through Jesus Christ, through whose body all reconciliation to God took place. Jesus is the head of the church; therefore our tithe belongs to the church.

> *Bring the whole tithe into the storehouse, that there may be food in my house.*
> **Malachi 3:10**

> *Bring the best of the firstfruits of your soil to the house of the Lord your God.*
> **Exodus 23:19**

If we take the position of deciding where our tithe belongs, if we decide to split up our ten per cent and give it to various organisations or charities, then we are taking ownership of it ourselves instead of acknowledging that it belongs to God. It is also important to remember that it does not matter whether the church is a 'good investment' or not, it does not matter what the church does with our money – God will be the judge of that. What is important is that when we bring the tithe into God's house it not only positions us under God's blessing, but it also honours God and supports the physical means of preaching the gospel.

To those serving God in the ministry

The Bible also commends giving to those who spread the gospel. In fact in Philippians 4:18 Paul calls the money sent to him from the Philippians a *"fragrant offering, an acceptable sacrifice, pleasing to God."* So let us, like the Philippians be generous with those who work for God be they our own elders, itinerant preachers or missionaries.

The King will reply, 'I tell you the truth, whatever you did for one of the least of these brothers of mine, you did for me.'

Matthew 25:40

To each other

In the early church we find that the spirit of generosity was so great that the believers started *"selling their possessions and goods"* and giving to anyone *"as he had need"* (Acts 2:45). Like the believers in the early church we are told quite clearly in the New Testament to look after others in God's house. Galatians 6:10 tells us, *"Therefore, as we have opportunity, let us do good to all people, especially to those who belong to the family of believers."* Doing *"good"* must surely include being generous and helping to meet the needs of others in the church. 1 John 3:17 also commends us to look after our fellow believers, *"If anyone has material possessions and sees his brother in need but has no pity on him, how can the love of God be in him?"* Verse 18 goes on to say; *"Dear children, let us not love with words or tongue but with actions and in truth."*

This I think leads us to the point of looking after our fellow church goers. Jesus says in John *"A new command I give you: Love one another. As I have loved you, so you must love one another. By this all men will know that you are my disciples, if you love one another"* (John 13:34-35). If we follow this commandment and love one another, with not just words but with actions, surely this will mean that we take care of one another in every way, including financially. If we do this and there are no needy persons among us (Acts 4:34), this will be the outward sign to the world that we love one another. This is what will make the church and Christianity different and appealing to the world. Maybe then we will become more like the early church where they *"enjoyed the favour of all the people. And the Lord added to their number daily those who were being saved"* (Acts 2:47).

He who is kind to the poor lends to the Lord, and he will reward him for what he has done.

Proverbs 19:17

The elders who direct the affairs of the church well are worthy of double honour, especially those whose work is preaching and teaching.

1 Timothy 5:17

To the poor

I didn't go to bed hungry last night, but conservative estimates are that 800 million people – that's more than 12 per cent of the world's people – go to bed hungry each night. That is overwhelming. The number is so great that it may leave us feeling hopeless about what we can do. But Scripture consistently emphasises our responsibility to give to the poor and the destitute. In fact the Bible reveals God's heart and concern regarding the poor in more than three hundred verses.

The parable of the Good Samaritan in Luke 10:25-37 serves to remind us that we should reach out and help those who are in need. Ignoring those whom God calls us to minister to is not a Kingdom option. In Deuteronomy we read, *"Give generously to him and do so without a grudging heart; then because of this the Lord your God will bless you in all your work and in everything you put your hand to. There will always be poor people in the land. Therefore I command you to be open-handed towards your brothers and towards the poor and needy in your land"* (Deuteronomy 15: 10-11). Isaiah, the prophet, declares God's commands to extend care to the poor in Isaiah chapter 58:10-11 saying, *"If you extend your soul to the hungry and satisfy the afflicted soul, then your light shall dawn in the darkness, and your darkness shall be as the noonday. The Lord will guide you continually, and satisfy your soul in drought, and strengthen your bones; you shall be like a watered garden, and like a spring of water, whose waters do not fail."*

Luke 12:33-34 says, *"Sell your possessions and give to the poor. Provide purses for yourselves that will not wear out, a treasure in heaven that will not be exhausted, where no thief comes near and no moth destroys. For where your treasure is, there your heart will be also."* So even though the scale of global poverty might make you think that you can't have any an impact, we need to give to the poor in obedience to God and together we might just make a difference. In fact, a Christian research organisation called *empty tomb, inc* published a report called "The state of church giving through 2003" in which they say that;

If members of historically Christian congregations in the USA had given at the 10% level in 2003, there would have been an additional $156 billion available. The potential impact of this money is seen in need statistics that could be addressed in Jesus' name: $5 billion could help stop the majority of 29,000 deaths a day around the globe among children under five, most of whom are dying from preventable poverty conditions; $7 billion could provide basic education for the world's children; $124 million could launch a massive word evangelism effort in the "10-40 Window" (area of global need).

So, if we each do our part, maybe together we will have the capacity to be God's hands and feet on the earth today.

He who bestows his goods upon the poor shall have as much again and ten times more.

John Bunyan, Preacher, 1628 – 1688

Day 13

AND IT SHALL BE GIVEN TO YOU

You shall give to him freely without begrudging it; because of this the Lord will bless you in all your work and in all you undertake.

Deuteronomy 15:10, AMP

God doesn't need your money, He is God. He can and does operate without your help. So why is there so much advice about money in the Bible? What does God want more than your money? He wants your heart to turn to Him so that He can bless you. God's motive in His command to us to give is not to benefit Him – it is to benefit us.

Giving strengthens your faith

It is very easy to get caught up thinking that "if I can please God, then..." But when we start thinking in this way we tend to overlook everything that God has already done for us. We try so hard to please God with our works that the hand of God becomes constrained. God doesn't want to reward our works as this is contrary to how we are meant to function. Deuteronomy 8:17-18 highlights this. It says, *"You may say to yourself, 'My power and the strength of my hands have produced this wealth for me.' But remember the Lord your God, for it is He who gives you the ability to produce wealth, and so confirms his covenant, which he swore to your forefathers, as it is today."*

The blessing of the Lord brings wealth, and he adds no trouble to it.

Proverbs 10:22

As we give back to God, it helps us to remember and be grateful for everything that God has done and continues to do for us. It reminds us that His supply has nothing to do with what we can or cannot do on our own. By choosing to give back to God we are making a tangible decision to have faith in His provision. We are making a choice, a commitment to rely on God and to stop trying to operate in self-sufficiency. After all God designed us to operate out of relationship with Him and He wants to be our supplier.

And my God will meet all your needs according to his glorious riches in Christ Jesus (Philippians 4:19).

Giving helps you to live in God's freedom

When we come to a place where we can rely on God and what He has does for us, it brings with it a sense of freedom; freedom from striving to do things in our own strength, with the futility of our own thinking. Generosity also helps to free us from destructive materialism and greed. We all know that money and the possibility of getting more money can sometimes exert a hold over us. Money can be a very powerful motivator, and it is easy to get caught up in going after more. Giving money through tithes and offerings will enable us to live contentedly under the riches of God's blessing - this is the antidote to becoming sidetracked by greed.

> *"No one can serve two masters. Either he will hate the one and love the other, or he will be devoted to the one and despise the other. You cannot serve both God and money."*
> **Matthew 6:24**

This sense of freedom does not happen when we give unless we act with the right understanding. If we find that we are giving through fear, because we think that our salvation is dependent on our giving, then we have misunderstood the biblical design for giving. It is faith in Jesus Christ and His death on the cross that seals our salvation. When we give we need to give voluntarily, as it says in Corinthians 9:, "*Each man should give what he has decided in his heart to give, not reluctantly or under compulsion, for God loves a cheerful giver.*" Paul then goes on to say in verse 8, "*And God is able to make all grace abound to you, so that in all things at all times, having all that you need, you will abound in every good work.*" We need to give from an understanding that God is our provider, not because we feel forced or coerced.

It is also important to remember that we shouldn't give to earn God's favour, and we shouldn't think that if we give that we are somehow better or holier than someone who doesn't. Tithing, giving, being generous, these are all free will decisions. Is there a penalty for not giving? Yes in as much as failure to

Then he said to them, "Watch out! Be on your guard against all kinds of greed; a man's life does not consist in the abundance of his possessions."
Luke 12:15

Give, and it will be given to you. A good measure, pressed down, shaken together and running over, will be poured into your lap. For with the measure you use, it will be measured to you.
Luke 6:38

do so diminishes our blessing and our potential for effective service and responsible stewardship.

We are also instructed in the Bible to give cheerfully (2 Corinthians 9:7), expectantly (Luke 6:8), sacrificially (2 Corinthians 8:2-3) and not for the purpose of earning man's favour (Matthew 6:2). Giving is truly a test of our hearts and it is only possible to tithe and be generous in the manner that God intended when we have a revelation of God's heart towards us, when we realise that there is an open heaven over us. When we tithe and give from the right perspective, we will be blessed of God and because of our right understanding, that blessing will flow through our lives to others and we will begin to fulfil the heart of God.

Day 14

WORK – PRODUCTIVITY AND INCOME

The average UK citizen can expect to live approximately 29,200 days, or 80 years. Despite what many people believe, work was introduced for our benefit in the sinless environment of the Garden of Eden – it is not a result of the fall of man. *"The Lord God placed the man in the Garden of Eden to tend and watch over it"* (Genesis 2:15, NLT). The very first thing that God did with Adam was to put him to work. God is always at work and He has created us to work.

Productivity and success

It is important to make those things that you plan happen. Almost everything you have in life comes as a result of your plans and productivity. Some are born with monetary advantages, or benefit from windfalls or rewards over which they have little or no control; but these are not the primary ingredients that give rise to a successful life. Productivity and success are dependent on one another. Productivity without a sense of accomplishment and contribution will eventually seem unimportant. At the same time, success will never be fully attained unless it is the result of outworking a plan thus giving rise to a sense of accomplishment.

Hard work is a thrill and a joy when you are in the will of God.

Robert A Cook, Evangelist and broadcaster 1912 – 1991

Components of productivity and success

Recognise who you work for. Paul tells us in Colossians 3:23-24 that we work for the Lord, *"Whatever you do, work at it with all your heart, as working for the Lord, not for men, since you know that you will receive an inheritance from the Lord as a reward. It is the Lord Christ you are serving."*

Although Joseph worked in Potipher's household, Genesis 39:2-3 makes it clear that, *"the Lord was with Joseph and he prospered, and he lived in the house of his Egyptian master. When his master saw that the Lord was with him and that the Lord gave him success in everything he did."* Joseph wasn't ready for the palace until he had been through the trials at Potipher's house and prison.

God gives promotion

You should recognise God's role in your promotion in the world, *"No one from the east or the west or from the desert can exalt a man. But it is God who judges: He brings one down, he exalts another"* (Exodus 75:6-7). This demonstrates the difference in the way Christians should think about work compared to the way the world thinks.

Shun discouragement at work

When workplace discouragement arises, we seem to lose energy and interest in productivity. Sometimes there is a sense of feeling lost or hopeless, or maybe even feeling worthless. Overcoming these feelings is sometimes easier said than done. Remember in Ephesians 2:10: *"We are God's workmanship."*

Employers

If you are an employer you will desire to see your employees blessed and successful. Employers have responsibilities, including:

And masters [employers], treat your slaves [employees] in the same way. Do not threaten them, since you know that he who is both their Master and yours is in heaven, and there is no favouritism with him.

Ephesians 6:9

- To lead fairly (Colossians 4:1)

- To communicate well and clearly (Genesis 11:6)

- To pay a fair wage (Malachi 3:5; Deuteronomy 24:14-15)

- To pray for godly employees for they are a blessing (Genesis 30:27; Genesis 39:4-5)

- Absolute honesty (Daniel 6:4)

Employees

If you are an employee your work responsibilities, include:

- Faithfulness (Daniel 6:10)

- Being a person of prayer (Daniel 6:21)

- Honouring his/her employer (Daniel 6:21)

- Honouring fellow employees (Proverbs 30:10)

- Communicating faith (Daniel 6:26)

Our work for Christ can be a common ground to reach others with the message of salvation – see 1 Corinthians 9:22. Whatever a person is like, I try to find common ground with him so that he will let me share with him. Do you see your workplace as a mission field? We have the opportunity and should share the good news of our faith.

A man can only do what he can do. But if he does that each day he can sleep at night and do it again the next day.

Albert Schweitzer

Should we be ambitious?

The Bible does not condemn ambition per se – indeed, Paul was ambitious: *"We make it our goal to please Him"* (2 Corinthians 5:9) – but the Bible does condemn selfish ambition: *"But if you have...selfish ambition in your heart, do not be arrogant and so lie against the truth. This wisdom is not that which comes down from above, but is earthly, natural, and demonic. For where...selfish ambition exists, there is disorder and every evil thing"* (James 3:14-16, NASB).

Thus the Bible is not against ambition, just the wrong type of ambition. Our ambition should be to please Christ.

Most of us struggle with too many things to do and too little time in which to do them. The good can become the enemy of the best. Once you have a clear vision of God's call on your life it becomes much easier to evaluate opportunities and say, 'No' to those who would distract you from what the Lord wants you to accomplish.

Whatever you do, do your work heartily as for the Lord rather than for men.... It is the Lord whom you serve"

Colossians 3:23-24, NASB

I shovel money out, and God shovels it back...but God has a bigger shovel!

**Industrialist
R G LeTourneau**

The purpose of any Christian in business is to glorify God, not just make a profit. One key to being faithful to the Lord is making decisions on the basis of God's Word and not on circumstances, feelings, or what is acceptable to society.

Larry Burkett, Co-Founder, Crown Financial Ministries, 1939-2003

I have two close friends. One has only average ability but because he has been single-minded in his focus has had an enormous impact. The other is much more capable but has scattered his energies pursuing numerous projects with limited success.

Someone once said, *"Work as unto the Lord...the pay may or may not be great, but the retirement benefits are out of this world!"* This is true, and you will find an additional benefit – increased satisfaction from a job done to the best of your ability.

Day 15

WORK AND BUSINESS

I enjoyed a career managing my own businesses for over 30 years. I had no formal business training and my only qualification was a professional one. Back when I started my first business, there were relatively few self-help books on managing a business so I learned to apply biblical management principles to my understanding of how to grow my business.

If you are a business owner or manager the Bible is replete with wisdom and principles that apply to how you manage and grow a business. After all, Jesus' earthly father was in business on his own account, and Jesus certainly grew up with the dynamics of business around him before he went full-time into "My Father's business."

A business owner or manager can apply the principles in this devotional to managing a business. For example, God owns your business (1 Chronicles 29:11-12). Indeed that is a very good place to start, as I know what it is like to see the business as *mine*!

There are four primary purposes for a business:

1. To glorify God

Business owners and managers should glorify God in their personal and business lives. In John 17:4, Jesus said, *"I have brought you glory on earth by completing the work you gave me to do."* The only way to glorify the Lord is to conduct our business according to the principles found in God's Word. Our work must be done without compromising God's ways.

Glorifying God in the business means dealing with employers, employees, suppliers, customers, and competitors as if we were dealing with Christ. Christian business leaders try to build win-win relationships, not just because it is good business

Work is not a curse, it is a blessing from God who calls man to rule the earth and transform it, so that the divine work of Creation may continue with man's intelligent efforts.

Pope John Paul 11

It is our best work that He wants, not the dregs of our exhaustion. I think He must prefer quality to quantity.

George MacDonald, Poet and Scottish Minister 1824-1905

All hard work brings a profit, but mere talk leads only to poverty.

Proverbs 14:23

----

practice, but because they care about other people. Besides glorifying God it also earns us the right to introduce others to the Saviour.

2. To make a profit

One of the outcomes of a business is to make a profit. There is no biblical admonition against making a profit. Profits are the result of a well-run business and should be considered both normal and honourable.

Unfortunately, there are many reasons why businesses fail to earn a profit. Some are unprofitable because they lack effective internal controls, some are disorganised, some are unable to attract good employees, some do not understand changes in their customers' needs, and some see their results slump due to external causes such as a recession.

Some businesses are not profitable because the owners choose to live beyond the means of their business. They go out of business because the owner draws a salary larger than the business can afford.

The commitment to being profitable means wisely building a business with a solid foundation and not allowing greed or presumption to put employees, investors, suppliers or creditors at undue risk. Although it is no sin to fail in business, business owners and managers should seek to conduct their business in ways that promote financial stability.

3. To support the work of Christ

There is a dependent relationship between those involved in Christian ministry and Christians in business – they need one another. This is not an accidental relationship; God designed it that way.

Paul wrote to the Roman church, *"Having then gifts differing according to the grace that is given to us, let us use them: if prophecy, let us prophesy in proportion to our faith; or ministry, let us use it in our ministering...he who gives, with liberality* (Romans 12:6-8, NKJV).

Giving is one of the purposes of Christians in business; it is what God has gifted them to do. When businessmen and women understand that they are strategic in contributing to the funding of the work of Christ, their work takes on eternal significance.

Come to me, all who labour and are heavy laden, and I will give you rest.

Matthew 11:28, RSV

----

4. To spiritually impact your sphere of influence

The Lord has given business owners and managers a position of influence in the workplace to impact co-workers, suppliers, customers, and even competitors. If you count the family members of everyone you impact, you may have a larger 'congregation' than many churches.

The Lord has appointed business owners to represent Him and bring His principles, values, love and presence into the workplace. The workplace provides a platform for evangelism, for discipleship, and for influencing others through serving and then sharing His message through words and actions.

The Bible has so much to say about running a business including leadership, finances, human resources, organisation, planning and marketing. We all serve an amazing God. You might not be a business owner or manager yourself but you can pray for those you know who are. Business owners have responsibilities and opportunities – pray that they may use them to extend His Kingdom here on earth.

The secret of your success is determined by your daily agenda...we over exaggerate yesterday, we overestimate tomorrow and we underestimate today.

John Maxwell

Day 16

THE STRANGLEHOLD OF DEBT

The recession that started in January 2009 was preceded by the credit crunch of 2007. Before then, in July 2004 the Bank of England announced that household borrowing had passed the £1 trillion mark, but just four years later that debt had spiralled to over £1.5 trillion. The growth in the economy had been sustained through a massive increase in debt combined with a buoyant stock market.

In the US, where many of the problems are believed to have started, unsecured debt had increased every year from 1952 (when records started) to 2008. Students are obliged to incur debt while in higher education and sadly many people are still in debt when they retire. Unsecured lending attracts the highest rate of interest, with rates ranging from 15 to 20 per cent, and store cards usually surpass these excessive rates. Never before had the failure of man's economy been so evident to so many. Debt also extracts a physical toll. It often increases stress, which contributes to mental, physical and emotional fatigue. It can stifle creativity and harm relationships.

How has debt taken such a hold?

The first credit card was introduced in this country in 1966. Until that time households did not have computers and payments were normally made using cash or cheques. In the ensuing years, however, technology has advanced relentlessly while consumerism has gained a stranglehold in many families. There are now so many more goods to buy and so much more that people want (as distinct from need).

Marketers tell us that we need something because, 'You're worth it,' and the Internet, cards, and PIN numbers facilitate the ready purchase of whatever we desire. With an economy that promotes easy access to credit and a materialist culture holding society in its grip, debt has become accepted and regarded as the norm. As a consequence, minds have become transformed and conformed to the ways of the world, leaving some people burying their heads in despair, overwhelmed by the problem of debt. How amazing that it took only four years for household debt in the UK to increase by 50 per cent!

Before the reduction in interest rates in 2008 the average household was paying approximately £4,000 p.a. in interest on their total debt. This reduced to just over £2,500 p.a. toward the end of 2009. That means that the average household is paying approximately 15 per cent of net income purely to service interest payments.

The Bible on debt

So what counsel can we find in the Bible concerning debt? Nowhere does the Bible command Christians not to assume debt, nor does Scripture say that debt is a sin, but the Bible does contain warnings about being in debt. Proverbs 22: 7 tells us that, "*the borrower is slave* [servant] *to the lender.*" Our monetary system is largely based on debt; it seems so natural to be in debt, but is that not to some extent a result of people succumbing to the world's temptations? Paul in 1 Corinthians 7:23 reminds us that, "*You were bought with a price; do not become slaves of men.*" The world's definition of debt is enjoying today those things that you cannot afford until tomorrow, in other words I want to enjoy instant gratification.

He that goes a borrowing goes a sorrowing.

Benjamin Franklin

The Apostle Paul again commands us to, "*present your bodies a living sacrifice, holy, acceptable to God, which is your reasonable service. And do not be conformed to this world, but be transformed by the renewing of your mind*" (Romans 12:1-2, NKJV).

Debt presumes upon tomorrow

When we get into debt we assume that we will earn enough in the future to pay it off. Scripture cautions us against making presumptions: "*Come now, you*

A man lacking in judgement strikes hands in pledge and puts up security for his neighbour.

Proverbs 17:18

who say, 'Today or tomorrow, we will go to this or that city, spend a year there, carry on business and make money'. Why, you do not even know what will happen tomorrow.... Instead you ought to say 'If it is the Lord's will, we will live and do this or that'" (James 4: 12-15, NKJV).

The blessings of becoming debt free go far beyond the financial area: they extend to the spiritual and marital realms. No one who is financially bound can be spiritually free.
Larry Burkett, Co Founder, Crown Financial Ministries, 1939-2003

Debt may deny God an opportunity

The obvious alternative to borrowing in order to make purchases is to save until you can afford to pay for it. There is a sense in which saving and preparing to spend provides a restraining discipline by deferring the time when you will benefit from whatever it is you wish to acquire. In that time your desire to make that purchase may either evaporate or turn into a greater sense of ownership as you know that when you have finished saving you can buy and enjoy.

On the other hand, there are those who have prayed and trusted God to provide. This provokes the question, does it require more faith to trust God to pay off our purchases made with debt or to wait on Him to provide before we make the purchase? It is important to understand that the Bible does not promise that He will fulfil our carnal desires or provide the luxuries of this world (1 John 2:15-17) or riches, (1 Timothy 6:9-10) all of which can be snares.

Say not my soul, "From whence
Can God relieve my care?"
Remember that Omnipotence
Has servants everywhere.
His method is sublime,
His heart profoundly kind;
God never is before His time,
And never is behind.
Thomas Toke Lynch, English congregational minister, 1818-1871

Day 17

WHEN DEBT MAY BE THE WAY

It is always important to read Scripture in context – the Bible does not say that debt is a sin. God loves us so much that He gives us many guidelines and instructions so that we may be wise in our ways. He does not condemn us when we find ourselves in a mess. On the contrary, He sent Jesus specifically to reach out to us whose lives are in a mess. He gave us the church as the body of Christ – not just a home for the redeemed, but a hospital for sinners!

When can we borrow?

The Bible is silent on when we can owe money. It warns against the dangers of debt, but does not preclude it. In my opinion it is possible to owe money for a home mortgage, to invest in a business, or to train for a career. However, we believe this is permissible only if the following four criteria are met:

How long will it take you to become debt free?

1. The item purchased is an asset with the potential to appreciate or produce income

2. The value of an item equals or exceeds the amount owed against it

3. The debt is not so high that repayment puts undue strain on your spending

4. The debt does not give rise to anxiety (Isaiah 32:17)

A home mortgage might meet the first requirement as, over time a house usually, but not always, appreciates. You can meet the second requirement by investing a reasonable deposit so that you would expect to sell the home for at least enough to repay the mortgage. The third requirement means buying an affordable house – one with a monthly repayment that does not strain your spending plan. Make sure you could continue to repay your mortgage even if the interest rates increased by two, or even three per cent and you have the necessary savings for unexpected cash requirements like repairs or maintenance.

A business owner may need to raise capital for the start or purchase of a business, or possibly to provide a source of working capital.

Student debt

Student loans started in the 1990/91 academic year and each year about 850,000 new students take out a student loan for the purposes of tuition fees and living costs. The average first year loan is more than £3,000 a year. By the time higher education is completed student debt may well be in excess of £20,000. This comprises student loan debt, bank debt, and other debt possibly to parents.

Generally students and their parents together face the challenge of how to finance the costs of higher education. Student debt is almost inevitable for those pursuing a degree, and although it is in some ways unique (you are unlikely to secure any other loan at such a low rate of interest or with repayments so directly linked to earnings) the debt is nevertheless a burden at the start of the working adult life. There is also a danger that it might lead to a belief that debt cannot be avoided, with a consequential lifestyle of debt that stretches to borrow the maximum that is affordable.

In some parts of the country people are not earning enough to repay the debt while generally student debt is not repaid until people reach their forties.

What is important is that students take a mature attitude to student debt, they plan and live to a realistic budget and where possible work to minimise their debts. Once leaving higher education the repayment of student debt should be a priority over seeking an even higher standard of living.

Do you have a financial roadmap?

We should not be like the Israelites who wandered in the wilderness for forty years on a journey that could have been done in 11 days (Deuteronomy 1:2) but rather we need to have a financial road map that will ensure that we do not repay debt for one day longer than is absolutely necessary. This is important as in some cases debt repayment may require many extra years even beyond retirement.

When debt has been the way

When should you not use debt? Resist the endeavours and strains of the companies who seek to tempt you with free credit – 'Buy today, pay tomorrow, only £x per month.' These and many similar offerings are the world's endeavours to snare you in debt.

Motor vehicles are often purchased using some form of debt finance. Here is an approach to breaking that cycle of car debt. When you have finished paying for your car resist the temptation to replace it, rather continue saving your monthly repayments and then when you have been doing this for two or three years you will be able to replace the car using the value of your car and the accumulated savings. You may not even have to use all you have set aside!

God opposes usury and greed, yet no one realises this because it is not simple murder and robbery.
Martin Luther, Theologian, 1483 – 1546

Consolidation loans are tempting because you are able to pay off your creditors with the loan and then make one payment instead of several. However you are likely to pay more interest in the long term and more than 50 per cent of those who consolidate their loans increase their debts with the 'spare' cash. Thus these loans only treat the 'symptoms' for a while but not the problem.
Larry Burkett

Make it your intention today to reduce your debt.

Day 18

BECOMING DEBT FREE – PART 1

Are you drowning in debt? Do you fear opening your post, or have you even stopped opening certain envelopes? Are you behind with your payments and receiving demands? Is your account being charged late payment fees? Is your expenditure greater than your income? Do you long for the day when your debts will be repaid and you will have peace of mind?

If any of these circumstances describes your situation it is time to rediscover your financial freedom. While you know that you are not alone, that is of little comfort as you recognise your part in getting into debt and acknowledge that you must now take action. Even if none of the above applies to you, you will almost certainly know someone who has debt, then pray for them as they work their way out of debt.

Today and tomorrow we seek to explore a biblical approach to becoming debt free by looking at twelve steps for getting out of debt.

Money talks...but all mine ever says is good-bye.

But before that can happen, you first need to make a decision that you will not incur one penny of additional debt; that the building up of the debt mountain has to stop. Perhaps today is the day to make that decision. And once you have made it, prepare to start thinking about saving!

Now we will look at the first six of twelve steps to becoming debt free:

1. Pray

In 2 Kings 4:1-7 we learn about the widow who was threatened with losing her children to her creditor and asked Elisha for help. Elisha instructed her to borrow many empty jars from her neighbours. The Lord then multiplied her only possession – a small amount of oil – and all her jars were filled. She then sold the oil and repaid her debts to free her children. The same God who provided supernaturally for the widow is interested in you becoming debt free. The first step is to pray and seek the Lord's help and guidance in your journey to become debt free. If you feel that you have borrowed beyond what was wise or necessary ask God to forgive you and to walk alongside you on the debt repayment journey.

2. Stop borrowing

This is a step that can be extraordinarily difficult to take. It requires you to decide that you will not increase your borrowing. You need to decide it is time to stop letting your borrowing get any further out of control. Some have taken that step with the help of plastic surgery – cutting up their cards! Others have frozen their cards in ice so that it would take time to retrieve them! If you are concerned about how you will get along without your credit cards, rest assured you can train yourself to be independent of those 850x550mm pieces of plastic debt inducers!

> *Credit and credit cards are not the problem; it is the misuse of credit that creates the problems. Four rules for using credit cards: never use them for anything other than budgeted purchases; pay them off every month; the first month you cannot pay the account, destroy the card and never use it again; keep in mind that just because you can afford something, you don't necessarily need it.*
>
> **Larry Burkett**

3. Record your expenditure

For the next month, record all your income and expenditure, down to the last penny – and note especially how you spend your cash. This requires discipline, but it is amazing how much more aware you will become of your spending habits and how sensitive you will become to reducing non-essential expenditure.

It usually takes time to get into debt. Increasing debt is like gaining weight – it results from indiscipline. Conversely, getting rid of debt is like shedding weight – it takes discipline! The excess debt pounds will be shed through more careful spending habits and diligently

For in the land the Lord your God is giving you to possess as your inheritance, he will richly bless you, if only you fully obey the Lord your God and are careful to follow all these commands I am giving you today. For the Lord your God will bless you as He has promised, and you will lend to many nations but will borrow from none. You will rule over many nations but none will rule over you.

Deuteronomy 15:4-6

The Crown Financial Ministries Practical Application Workbook can help you with this.

www.crownuk.org

monitoring your expenditure. At the end of the month, total up your expenditure. Now you have some of the essential information for a needs-based (monthly or weekly) budget.

4. Your budget will unlock the keys to debt reduction

Your daily devotional is not the right time to start preparing a budget, but it does provide an opportunity to examine your heart before God and to determine not to allow your future spending to be influenced so much by the world's materialistic paths. Remember that you are a steward of what you have been entrusted with. Ask yourself if and how you need to make changes to your spending patterns. How can you pare down your expenditure so that you can *invest* more in reducing your debt? As you meditate on these matters it is important to stay focussed on Christ and to trust in Him. Remember it took time to get into debt and it will probably take time to become debt free.

If you need help to prepare a budget see pages 95–99 in the appendix.

5. List what you own

Repaying debt is a great investment.

Evaluate your possessions to determine if there is anything you do not need that you could sell to help you get out of debt more quickly. What about the clothes you no longer wear or the technology you no longer use?

6. List what you owe

Many people do not know exactly what they owe, particularly if they owe a lot. Perhaps this is an aspect of human nature to avoid unpleasant things in the hope they will go away. In any event, you need to list your debts to determine your current financial position.

Tomorrow we will look at the final six steps to becoming debt free.

Day 19

BECOMING DEBT FREE – PART 2

Paul informs the believers in the church at Corinth that, "*their bodies were bought at a price; do not become slaves of men*" (1 Corinthians 7: 23). You will recall that Proverbs 22:7 reads, "*Just as the rich rule the poor, so the borrower is servant to the lender*" (TLB).

Why does the Lord not want us to become slaves to debt? Maybe it is because the debt and materialism in the 21st century competes with Him who we know is a jealous God. Maybe it is because the battles that we face are spiritual battles. When we are slaves to debt we are not as free to serve God or to fight the good fight. When our minds are fixed on the pleasures and technology of this world, they are not fixed on Him. When our lives are so committed to servicing debt we may find that Satan has us in a place where we are ineffective as ambassadors for Christ.

Again, Paul in his first letter to the church at Corinth reminded believers that their bodies were a temple of the Holy Spirit, whom they had received from God. Paul wrote, "*You were bought at a price. Therefore honour God with your body*" (1 Corinthians 6:20). Let us recognise that getting out of debt is part of a battle that is not just being fought here on earth. Any debt mortgages the future as it presumes upon tomorrow and assumes that you will have the income to repay what is owed.

Continuing with the twelve steps on your path to freedom from debt:

7. Establish a debt repayment plan
There are a number of accepted approaches to repaying debt. One that is effective and popular is the 'debt snowball' approach.

A big part of being strong financially is that you know where you are weak and take action to make sure you don't fall prey to the weakness. And we all are weak.

Dave Ramsey, US radio talk show host

Neither a borrower not a lender be; for loan oft loses both itself and friend, and borrowing dulls the edge of husbandry.

Shakespeare, Hamlet

Download a snowball calculator from My Crown.

www.crownuk.org

With this approach, you list your debts with the smallest first and largest last. Then, you repay the minimum amount on all debts with the exception of the smallest, on which you repay as much as you can – and as quickly as possible. When it is repaid, roll the monthly/weekly amount you were repaying on that debt and add it to the amount you are paying off on the second debt. In this way your repayments will snowball from debt to debt.

8. Consider earning additional income

Many people hold jobs that simply do not pay enough to meet their needs, even if they spend wisely. If you are able to earn additional income, decide in advance to use it to pay off debts. Whether we earn much or little, we tend to spend more than we make, so be careful not to fall into the trap of spending the extra income. Remember that word of instruction from Ecclesiastes 5:10: *"whoever loves money never has money enough."*

> *Christians who are trapped by borrowing have violated one or more of the scriptural principles God has given. He says that when someone borrows, he or she becomes a servant to the lender; the lender becomes an authority over the borrower. This clearly defines God's attitude about borrowing.*
> **Larry Burkett**

9. Be content with what you have

The advertising industry uses powerful methods to persuade people to buy. Frequently the message is intended to create discontent with what we have. Television, the Internet, and magazines all resonate with the message that we need to buy more 'stuff' – 'because you deserve it.'

You are only poor when you want more than you have.

In the consumer-driven economy:

- *The more television you watch, especially the shopping channels, the more you spend.*

- *The more you look at catalogues, magazines, door leaflets, Internet banner advertisements etc, the more you spend.*

- The more you shop, the more you spend.

It is probably something to do with the way we have all become wired because we are so accustomed to spending. Some even regard it as therapy! Paul writes, "*But godliness with contentment is great gain*" (1 Timothy 6:6). It is godly to be content and not always having something that we think we "must" buy. Someone who is addicted to drugs must have the next fix. In a similar way, our lack of contentment can be assuaged only by another dose of buying (even if we do not have the funds to actually spend).

10. Consider a change in lifestyle

Some might decide they have to lower their standard of living to become debt free while others might sell a home and move to a smaller one, or even move to rented accommodation. As tough a decision as it might be, some people have transferred their children from private education to a state school. In short, they have temporarily sacrificed their standard of living or preferred options to be debt free in as short a time as possible. Then they achieve the financial freedom to really enjoy living again.

The wicked borrows and does not repay, but the righteous shows mercy and gives.

Psalm 37:21, NKJV

11. Pray

I end where we started by encouraging you at all times to submit your finances to God. With over 2,300 verses – about seven and a half per cent of the Bible – referring to financial matters, there is much wisdom in God's Word and now that you have started on the road to getting out of debt I encourage you to continue the journey to biblical financial freedom. Spend much time in prayer, you will be given wisdom for your day including the ability to resist the temptation of debt or inappropriate spending. Jesus said, "*Get up and pray so that you will not fall into temptation*" (Luke 22:46). Prayer unlocks the power of God to work on our behalf.

12. And finally – love for the day is near

Paul charges the church at Rome to, "*Let no debt remain outstanding, except the continuing debt to love one another, for he who loves his fellowman has fulfilled the law*" (Romans 13:8).

Day 20

TOUGH TIMES DON'T LAST

Money issues are a common component of 'tough times.' At the very least, the lack of money, or even of money and possessions themselves, often feature in these situations. Having too much can give rise to sleepless nights trying to protect, manage or grow what you have, whereas having too little can result in losing sleep trying to balance the budget and respond to the red demand letters. Having 'nothing' or being in debt makes people feel destitute and often a burden on family or the government. Proverbs puts it like this: *"...give me neither poverty nor riches, but give me only my daily bread. Otherwise, I may have too much and disown you and say, 'Who is the Lord?' Or I may become poor and steal, and so dishonour the name of my God"* (Proverbs 30:8-9).

Whatever the cause, if you cannot do what you want, when you want and where you want, frustration or anxiety arises, and this is often a precursor to stress, which can be debilitating and develop into illness, either physical, mental or both. Thus, those journeying through 'tough times' can experience seemingly insurmountable pain and this is a major factor in the distress and helplessness experienced. People respond in different ways – some seek a quick fix while others might be in denial, burying their heads in the sand unable to address the situation.

Consider it pure joy, my brothers, whenever you face trials of many kinds, because you know that the testing of your faith develops perseverance.

James 1:2-3

Seeking God's solution

The most common response is a quick fix or an early exit from the problem. This leaves open the possibility that the root issue is not fully addressed or that not all the lessons are learned. Then there is a danger that the problem will repeat itself when the abyss of 'tough times' once again opens up ahead of the weakness reappearing or recurring.

The Bible teaches us to stand with our focus on God. Paul tells us to, 'put on the whole armour of God,' (Ephesians 6:11, 13, NKJV). We are reminded twice to put on the whole armour because we are prone to not using it all because the whole armour may restrict our movement more than we desire. Matthew 6:33 instructs us to, "seek first his Kingdom and his righteousness." Do not succumb, but allow his Word to help you overcome the enemy of debt or the giant of overwhelming debt. Prayerfully seek God's counsel. However long it takes, keep praying ceaselessly until the Lord God answers. It could be that the 'tough times' are a result of an unexpected event, such as an unexpected car or household expense, the death of a loved one, or they may be the culmination of years of wrong living or neglect. These are faith-testing times and opportunities to reach out and find God in your situation – and be assured He is there even before you.

> *Difficulties are God's errands; and when we are sent them we should esteem it a proof of God's confidence – as a compliment from God.*
> **Henry Ward Beecher, Clergyman, 1813-1887**

His oath, His covenant, His blood,
Support me in the raging flood;
When every earthly prop gives way,
He still is all my strength and stay.
Edward Mote, Hymn writer and English pastor, 1797 – 1874

The times will surely pass

Declare in both your head and your heart that the situation is not permanent. It will surely pass, so what you do and how you respond is important. Patience is a shock absorber at such times. Do not be quick to make a decision. It is always best to avoid making decisions in the eye of a storm if you can. Hindsight often clarifies that a hasty action or decision was not the right course of action. The disciples were in fear when in the dark of the night they thought the storm held danger. Jesus reassured them and spoke calm into their minds.

You may sleep on an empty stomach but you will not die! People have been known to live without food for weeks, while others have managed without electricity for most of their lives. As surely as spring follows winter, it is a season and it too will pass. Learn the lessons of the seasons so that you can help others when they face similar circumstances

> *Tough times don't last, but people do.*

Character cannot be developed in ease and quiet. Only through experience of trial and suffering can the soul be strengthened, vision cleared, ambition inspired and success achieved.

Helen Keller, 1880 – 1968

- -

The lowest ebb is the turn of the tide for there has never been a sunset yet, not followed by a sunrise.

- -

Therefore put on the full armour of God, so that when the day of evil comes, you may be able to stand your ground, and after you have done everything, to stand.

Ephesians 6:13

- -

and determine, so far as you are able to, not to walk through a time such as this again – or if you do, to know with godly assurance how to overcome what crosses your life's path.

Lessons to be learned

Tough times have many lessons to teach, and in most cases we desperately need those lessons. The author, broadcaster and missionary Elisabeth Elliot alludes to this in her statement, *"I am not a theologian or a scholar but I am very aware of the fact that pain is necessary to all of us, and tough times carry with them a great degree of pain. Out of the deepest pain comes the strongest conviction of the presence and the love of God."*

Allow God to speak to you clearly and hear the still small voice of calm that reassures you of His love. He speaks through His Word, the Bible, so look there *first* for answers. He once stood knocking at the door of your life waiting to be asked in. He *is still* with you and has given you the indwelling power and presence of his Holy Spirit; He is still waiting for you to invite Him into the situation you are in.

There is a way out of every tough situation. It is easier when we focus on God – He is our loving heavenly Father who seeks to bless us and teach us. Job learned of God's love in the adversities he faced. Learn what God has to teach you and ensure you do not blame God for those 'tough time' situations.

If we are quick to run to the bank manager, the credit card, our parents or aid agencies, we only lengthen our training period. For the children of Israel that meant forty years. But they came through in the end! Tough times are not a permanent phenomenon; they are temporary, so learn to see them as such.

How would you measure the amount of trust you have in God during tough times? Is it total, complete, unconditional, or is it limited by your view of your circumstances? God's Word says, *"Trust in the Lord with all your heart and do not lean on your own understanding. In all your ways acknowledge Him, and He will make your paths straight"* (Proverbs 3:5-6, NKJV).

Every humiliation, everything that tries and vexes us, is God's way of cutting a deeper channel in us through which the life of Christ can flow.
Oswald Chambers, Scottish Christian minister, 1874-1917

Day 21

HONOURING FINANCIAL COMMITMENTS

Living on credit and not repaying what is owed is characteristic of the wicked. Psalm 37:21 says, "*The wicked borrow and do not repay, but the righteous give generously.*" Christians should not behave in the same manner as 'the wicked.' Malachi records this, "*I will be quick to testify against...those who defraud labourers of their wages*" (Malachi 3:5) and this certainly also applies to those who have provided goods and services to us.

In bankruptcy, a court of law declares that a person is unable to pay his debts. Depending upon the type of bankruptcy, the court will either allow the debtor to develop a plan to repay his creditors or it will distribute his or her property among the creditors as payment for the debts. These modern bankruptcy procedures, including IVAs (Independent Voluntary Arrangements) provide a level of balanced legal protection for both the creditor and debtor. On the one hand, creditors have a fair entitlement to the debtor's assets if they have any. On the other, the law carries the benevolent intent of providing protection for the debtor with the objective that they can recover from the financial obligations and make a fresh start. Unfortunately, the system is subject to significant abuse and is often manipulated for unjust ends. Our obligations as followers of Christ are to obey His commands to us and the principles understood here tell us to not defraud others or avoid paying those debts we incur.

Often all it takes to start down the road to bankruptcy is a small raise or increase in income.

Mark Lloydbottom

Is bankruptcy wrong? No, the law serves to protect the debtor and creditor.

Do all that you can to repay what is legitimately owed and gain victory over your debt.

Should a Christian declare bankruptcy?

This is not a question with an easy 'Yes' or 'No' answer, for the Bible does not directly address the issue. With so many people finding bankruptcy a necessary route it is important for any Christian contemplating this to consider how to apply Christian principles to their financial situation.

We have the responsibility to keep our promises and pay what we owe. Ecclesiastes 5: 4-5 says, *"When you make a vow to God, do not delay in fulfilling it. He has no pleasure in fools; fulfil your vow. It is better not to vow than to make a vow and not fulfil it."*

This principle is reiterated by Paul in Romans 13:8: *"Let no debt remain outstanding."* This verse does not prohibit the believer from incurring debts but it does suggest that when you do so you are entering into a legal agreement and spiritual commitment to repay the debt in a timely and honest manner.

> *Bankruptcy is a serious matter and, at best, both sides lose. The creditors lose much of the money they are owed, and the debtors lose much of the respect they previously had. A person who has filed for bankruptcy can turn a negative situation into a positive one by making a commitment to repay what is legitimately owed. God's Word clearly says that a believer should be responsible for his or her promises and repay what is owed.*
> **Larry Burkett**

Seeking bankruptcy or an IVA should not be considered lightly. Psalm 37:21 tells us: *"The wicked borrow and do not repay, but the righteous give generously"* and this surely applies to borrowing with no intent or no concerted effort to repay. However, in my opinion bankruptcy is permissible in three circumstances:

1. Where a creditor forces a person into bankruptcy.

2. When the borrower experiences such extreme financial difficulties that there is no other option. There are occasions when the financial challenges become too extreme to reverse and bankruptcy is the only viable option. Even so,

this option should be exercised only after all others have been explored.

3. If the emotional health of the borrower is at stake because of an inability to cope with the pressure of aggressive creditors.

For example, if a husband deserts his wife and children leaving her responsible for business or household debts, she may not have the resources or income to meet these obligations.

After a person goes through bankruptcy they should seek counsel from a competent solicitor to determine if it is legally permissible to repay the debt, even though they are not obliged to do so. If it is allowable, they should make every effort to repay it. For a large debt, this may be a long-term goal that is largely dependent upon the Lord supernaturally providing the resources. Your obedience here might allow God to show you favour in ways that you do not understand or expect: He really does bless obedience.

Guaranteeing the debt of others

Have you guaranteed the debt of others? A person who guarantees becomes legally responsible for that debt. It is just as if you went to the bank, borrowed the money and gave it to your friend or relative who is asking you to guarantee.

Research in the US by the Fed-Trade commission reveals 50 per cent of those who guaranteed bank loans ended up making payments. Seventy-five per cent of those who guarantee for finance company loans ended up making payments. Fortunately, scripture speaks very clearly about guaranteeing. Proverbs 17:18 reads *"it's poor judgement to guarantee another person's debt or put up security for a friend"* (NLT).

Do not withhold good from those who deserve it, when it is in your power to act. Do not say to your neighbour, "Come back later; I'll give it tomorrow" when you now have it with you.

Proverbs 3:27-28

Day 22

MARRIAGE AND MONEY

There is a powerful relationship between our true spiritual condition and our attitude and actions concerning money and possessions.

Randy Alcorn

Money problems are a common cause or major contributory ingredient in marriage breakdown. My former Pastor, Johnny Hunt, says the two primary causes of marital breakup are money and lack of communication and the reason they are not communicating is because of money problems.

The exponential growth in secured and unsecured debt over the past forty years has fed an increasingly materialistic society with a 'have it, and have it now' mentality – buying on credit, paying later or stretching the home loan. There is no age barrier to this debt-creep – even those who are retired are not as free of debt as they once might have envisaged.

The financial quagmire that many households face is exacerbated by investments that rise only to plummet and a 'retirement pot' that is often inadequate. Thus the seeds of anxiety and discord are never far from the front door. To make matters worse, it is quite possible that the handling of money did not receive more than a few brief mentions when you lived at home – and if *you* have children that may still be the case.

Transforming your thinking

Like a course of treatment, it is important that you stay aligned as the canvas of what the Bible has to say about your finances becomes your own masterpiece. When you married you made a covenant with one another and as you did so you became 'one flesh', so if you are reading this and your spouse is not, then lovingly encourage him/her to join with you by reading these *Biblical Finance* devotionals. The way forward is not found in simply implementing a financial plan, but in allowing the word of God to transform your thinking and your

The challenge for most people is that their earning capacity does not match their yearning capacity.

planning. Rediscover the joy of communicating about these matters with one another – and, if you have children, plan how you can help them because the challenges when they leave home may be greater than ever before.

The majority of warnings in Christ's messages were to the wealthy, not the poor. Just having an abundance is not a sign of God's blessings. A disciplined lifestyle with an abundance is greater witness than the abundance could ever be.
Larry Burkett

Taking some practical steps

Here are some steps that I hope will help – they work for others, so why not you?

Step 1: Plan to do this together

Often one spouse takes responsibility for the finances. I am an accountant and have owned three businesses, yet my wife, who has no bookkeeping qualifications, masterminds our finances – pretty much from A to Z. A word to the spouse who is stronger in this area – do not dominate or get frustrated if your partner is not as good at this as you are. Do what you can to lovingly help your partner understand the household's finances.

You make deposits in your spouse's trust account by good communication, honesty, and transparency with money.

Howard Dayton

Step 2: Pray

I recommend you both get on your knees and pray. It is not that God will not hear your prayers if you do not, but rather you are giving God the honour He deserves – as you bend your knees you are submitting your will to Him as you both draw close to Him, and so to one another.

Step 3: Status

I strongly recommend that you each take five minutes to write down what state you think your finances are in – what needs fixing and what does not. Alongside each statement you might write a number from 1 (easy) to 5 (very difficult) to indicate how difficult a situation it is to address. You might also wish to add another column for the number of months/years you think it will take to change the situation. Then compare what you have each written and prepare a combined status report to see where you are in agreement and where there are differences in how you see the situation – or perhaps where there might

The effects of financial bondage on a marriage relationship are measurable in the statistics of failed marriages. A marriage is a partnership – much like the right and left hands of the same person. God's Word says that two people become one.

Larry Burkett

And if a Kingdom be divided against itself, that Kingdom cannot stand. And if a house be divided against itself, that house will not be able to stand.

Mark 3:24-25

----

be some 'blind spots.' Throughout, make sure you remain positive and share together as humbly as you do when you pray.

Step 4: Pray again!
Find time for one another – enjoy each other's company.

Next step
The Crown Financial Ministries *Practical Application Workbook* provides all the instructions you need to develop a balanced spending plan as well as a wide range of personal planning steps. Also available are story-study books for children and adult biblical financial studies that teach what the Bible has to say about how we handle our money and possessions.

> *I have watched over 100,000 families over my years of investment counselling. I always saw greater prosperity and happiness among those families who tithed than among those who didn't.*
> **Sir John Templeton, Investor and philanthropist, 1912-2008**

There is also a section in the appendix on 'How to Budget' starting on page 95.

Day 23

TRAINING OUR CHILDREN – PART 1

If you have children God has given you a tremendous opportunity and responsibility to nurture them and allow Him to use you to shape and mould them into all God desires for them.

Our materialistic, 'have it now' society impacts and influences each of us. Children today are affected by a range of external factors, including advertisements, the Internet, media stars, peers and so on. Whatever influences your children probably also influences their spending 'requests.'

I have heard so many parents tell me that they never spent time training their children how to handle money. Sometimes that was because the parents had money problems of their own. Children learn by example and although you might not feel you are qualified, you are – because you are the parents! Our children need training, shaping and moulding more than ever before – and not only in how to handle money.

Nurturing your children

Every child has his or her own God-given gifts and strengths, and it is a parent's responsibility to help the child identify these and encourage their development. One of the ways we can help our children is to teach them how to be good stewards of the resources God provides. If this is done properly, God can use parents to leave a legacy of faith to our children.

How do we do it? How do we teach them to be good stewards?

Train up a child in the way he should go, and when he is old he will not depart from it.

Proverbs 22:6, NKJV

A child who is allowed to be disrespectful to his parents will not have true respect for anyone.

Billy Graham

Love

Share the love of Jesus and set an example by loving your spouse, family and others. In fact Paul tells us to, *"Let him who boasts boast in the Lord"* (1 Corinthians 1: 31). We should share the truth of God's love and ways whenever we can. We should be a constant source of love and encouragement for our children. Think of it as being your children's greatest fan. Yes, there is a time for discipline, but there is also a time for encouragement.

If our children know that we truly love them they will be more willing to let us lead them and speak truth into their lives. Look at 1 Corinthians 13: 4-6 for the characteristics of love and ask yourself if you are displaying this kind of love to your children. Do your children know they are more important than your job, your standard of living, your hobbies? Take time to show your love and invest in them.

Provide

Many of the financial decisions we make now will affect our children in the future, so we need to make sure our children's needs are factored into our decision-making. Possible areas for consideration include education, weddings and perhaps assistance with initial housing costs.

This does not mean that we should provide every pound for every activity our child does, rather that we need to have a plan in place to provide for their needs. You and your spouse may decide that you want to earn more money to help pay for some of their needs. Teaching them the value of work is important.

Model

When Paul was talking to the church at Corinth and encouraging them to be more Christ-like, he said these words recorded in 1 Corinthians 11:1, *"Follow my example, as I follow the example of Christ."* Paul realised the importance of being a model, an example, of what he was teaching. The same thing goes for our children. In most cases, what we do will have a greater impact than what we say. James Dobson wrote, *"When children are young, they follow our advice, when they are older, they follow our example."* Our instruction will not be effective if we do not model it.

Parents cannot establish financial discipline in their children if they themselves are undisciplined. Teach your children that everyone needs to live on a budget. Children who have been taught the basic principles of money management early and have proved their ability to use them wisely could be trusted to handle a debit or credit card with no problem.

Larry Burkett

If your children followed your example today, what condition would they be in tomorrow? Would your example prepare them to be good stewards when they grow up, or would it cause them to make some of the mistakes you may have made?

Do not lose hope! Even if you have not started out right and modelled for your children the proper way to give, save and spend in a manner that honours God, you can always start today!

I have chosen him, so that he will direct his children and his household after him to keep the way of the Lord by doing what is right and just.

Genesis 18:19

Day
24

TRAINING OUR CHILDREN – PART 2

Training our children to be good stewards

When athletes train for the Olympic games they have an instructor to help them develop and oversee fitness, diet, technique, strength, focus and any necessary sport-specific requirements. The athletes benefit from that instruction as their skills are honed and their abilities sharpened with the aim of peaking at the Olympics.

We are to train our children so that as they grow they will not depart from the path we lay down. Our training is like the railway lines over which the train reaches its destination, time and time again. We teach them the paths so that they will unerringly follow. *"He leads me in the paths of righteousness"* (Psalm 23:3).

Train but do not exasperate

Fathers, do not exasperate your children; instead, bring them up in the training and instruction of the Lord.

Ephesians 6:4

In those well-known verses in Ephesians 6:1-3, Paul instructs children to obey their parents. However, in verse 4 fathers are instructed not to exasperate their children. Our children learn discipline and respect by being instructed in the ways of the Lord. Trying to discipline and command respect from our children without bringing them up in the training and instruction of the Lord only exasperates them.

One of the areas that is extremely important to instruct children in is how to be good stewards of the resources that God gives them and will provide for them in the future. If children are not prepared, they will have a difficult time managing money and other resources. If we do not teach them, the likelihood is that marketers and advertisers will!

Recognise

In our society, children have a large amount of disposable income as well as a persuasive influence in a significant number of family purchases. In fact, children are a powerful group of consumers on whom marketing and advertising companies spend seemingly endless budgets trying to capture their money – many times what is captured is the child's heart.

What to teach them

We must teach children what to value, including the importance of having a relationship with God. We should also teach them about having a balance between, family, work and ministry. Stewardship is also essential – the practical principles of giving, spending, saving, having a spending budget, and who owns everything.

We should teach them how to make good spending decisions. Children need to understand that, as they grow up, the chances are they will not have enough money to buy everything they want. You do your children a disservice if you do not teach them to wait. It is better to learn this in the safety of the family rather than in the prison of financial bondage. Purchasing something that has been planned for some time and savoured is a lesson they can draw on in adulthood. They must choose based on what is most important to them. You may teach them about budgeting for eating out and other forms of entertainment such as the cinema. For many families this is the highest cost in the family after all the 'essential' household costs have been accounted for – discuss an appropriate approach to optional expenditure.

Teaching topics

Teach the value of working hard and seeing work as a privilege and positive experience: *"All hard work brings a profit, but mere talk leads only to poverty"* (Proverbs 14:23). Make sure they know that money does not grow on trees.

Observing their parents, two children were heard to argue about where money came from. One thought it came from the cash machine while the other insisted it came from the supermarket cashier, who was always offering cash-back!

Teach them the value of saving and earning interest: *"Go to the ant...consider its ways and be wise...it stores its provision in summer and gathers its food at harvest"* (Proverbs 6:6-8). Watch how your children buy with money given to them as opposed to money they have earned. They are usually more responsible with the latter.

Teach them about taxes – how they are collected and how they are spent. They may not pay income tax yet, but they will almost certainly pay VAT.

Teach them about credit cards and loans. You could do this by loaning them money for something and charging them interest. You may wish to share with them about your own debt repayments at some stage.

Teach them the importance of tithing and giving. Teach them the appropriate way to receive gifts – with a thankful heart. Teach them about the importance of having goals and dreams.

If you wish to leave much wealth to your children, leave them in God's care. Do not leave them riches, but virtue and skill.

Saint John Chrysostom, AD 390

Day 25

FINANCES AND PREPARING FOR RETIREMENT

Think back to an event that occurred ten years ago. Can you remember the day you left school or your first day at work? Are these events you can recall with ease? As you go through childhood, adolescence, the teen years and into work, marriage, home and children, the end of working life draws ever closer. What will you need to live on when you no longer go to work? What income will you receive from your pension – and when?

Unless poverty is your preferred choice, saving for retirement is a necessity. Many do not save at all, and for those who do, it is probable that their investments will not generate the income they expect or require. How does your faith interplay with your planning for the future and how do you ensure that your planning is adequate?

Plan your finances beyond retirement

Retirement is the point you reach in life when you no longer receive remuneration for what you do. Retirement planning can dominate the thinking of Christians who have sizeable incomes, resulting in overkill in this area. The fear of having to do without in the future causes many to rob God's work of the very funds He has provided. This money is salted away into pension funds for twenty to forty years. God's Word does not prohibit but rather encourages saving for the future. As the Bible reads in Proverbs 21:20, "*In the house of the wise are stores of choice food and oil, but a foolish man devours all he has,*" but the example of the rich fool given by the Lord in

Plan ahead – it wasn't raining when Noah built the ark.

A little sleep, a little slumber, a little folding of the hands to rest and poverty will come on you like a bandit and scarcity like an armed man.

Proverbs 24:33-34

- -

Retirement may be an ending, a closing, but it is also a new beginning.

Catherine Pulsifer

- -

Luke 12:16-20 should be a clear direction that God's balance is – 'When in doubt – give; don't hoard.'

It all belongs to Him

Whatever the size of your retirement provision it is important to remember that it all belongs to Him. Be sensitive to the inner prompting of the Holy Spirit and avoid the temptation to think, 'it's mine and I couldn't live without it.' Some day you may feel led to give more of it away, or none of it that is between you and God. None of us will miss that final appointment when we meet Him face to face and give an account of our stewardship.

Does that sound foolish? I know young missionary couples serving the Lord who have invested everything to reach out and pursue their part in fulfilling the Great Commission. Remember that God commended the widow for giving away her last two pennies. He may or may not call you to give everything, but it is my experience that if you ask Him and listen you will hear Him calling. What a privilege to make an investment into a 'retirement home' that will last forever!

Of all the daily topics we look at together this is perhaps the one to which an entire book could be devoted. Listen to a financial adviser and you will almost certainly hear that you do not have enough. Markets may plummet, interest and annuity rates may be historically low – all seemingly justification for salting more away. It is when you look at areas of your life such as income in retirement that you should remember that the wealth you are looking at is based on man's economy – and that this does not work!

A look back at the effect of the recession that officially started in January 2009 serves as a reminder of what we read in Proverbs 23:5, "*Cast but a glance at riches, and they are gone, for they will surely sprout wings and fly off to the sky like an eagle.*" The portfolios of many are decimated when markets fall – and eventually they do fall! And many people approaching retirement find they are not worth what they thought and that their trust is perhaps not as fully in Him as they thought. Ecclesiastes 5:10 tells us clearly, "*Whoever loves money never has money enough; whoever loves wealth is never satisfied with his income. This too is meaningless.*"

Silence on the golden years?

If you search the Bible for an understanding of God's instruction for you in the 'retirement years' you will find nothing. Some choose to continue working to 'boost their income.' Of course, it is legitimate to plan for retirement, but beware of allowing the golf course or more leisure time to become your goal for retirement.

> *Retirement for Christians should mean freeing time to devote to serving others more fully without the necessity of getting paid for it. If Christian retirees have this motivation in mind while looking forward to retirement, then the Lord really will find us doing His work when He returns.*
> **Larry Burkett**

Retirement provides an opportunity to work as a volunteer. Make yourself available to God and there will never be a work shortage. We live in a lost and needy world. We are surrounded by people who are destined for hell. Plan your finances for retirement, but do not forget to ask God how He can use you and your retirement finances to further His Kingdom, after all it is only His Kingdom that lasts forever.

A retirement is a terrible thing to waste.

Day 26

PLANNING TO LEAVE AN INHERITANCE

It is my happiness that I have served Him who never fails to reward His servants to the full extent of His promise.

John Calvin

There is no advantage in being the richest man in the cemetery.

Colonel Sanders

Making a Will is not everyone's first choice activity – in fact it is reported that only one in seven adults has a Will. Do you have a Will and does it reflect your current intentions?

In that it sets out His plan for the heavens and the earth, the Bible is God's Will, his covenant of redemption through Jesus Christ, and his plan for our inheritance.

The Old Testament has many stories of how wealth was handed down from one generation to the next. In Genesis 12:7 God appeared to Abraham and promised his offspring the land of Canaan (Israel). Abraham left everything he owned to his eldest son Isaac. Solomon inherited great wealth from his father King David (1 Kings 9:4-7). He too prospered and when he died his wealth passed to his eldest son, Rehoboam.

We will all die. As Isaiah told King Hezekiah, "*This is what the Lord says: Put your house in order, because you are going to die; you will not recover*" (Isaiah 38:1). Unlike in the days of King Tutankhamen when they believed that wealth would be available in the afterlife, we know that "*Naked I came from my mother's womb, and naked I will depart*" (Job 1:21). We also know that someone else will inherit what we leave behind, "*I [Solomon] must leave it to the man who will come after me. And who knows whether he will be a wise man or a fool? Yet he will have control over all the fruit of my labour*" (Ecclesiastes 2:18-19, NKJV).

Who benefits?

We can only decide *before* we die who receives our wealth *after* we die. Recognising that passing on their wealth intact might not be a wise imposition on their children, these days the very rich may establish a charitable foundation, while others may leave relatively little, and some leave nothing but debts!

It is normal for spousal Wills to provide for the transfer of the major wealth to the surviving spouse. Nevertheless Scripture gives instruction in a number of areas including our children and grandchildren.

Children: the Bible makes it clear that parents should leave an inheritance to their children. The Bible contains many examples of parents passing on an inheritance and Paul in 2 Corinthians 12:14 instructs us that, "*children should not have to save up for their parents, but parents for their children.*" Again in 1 Timothy 5:8 Paul says that, "*If anyone does not provide for his relatives, and especially for his immediate family, he has denied the faith and is worse than an unbeliever.*"

Grandchildren: Proverbs tells us that "*Children's children are a crown to the aged, and parents are the pride of their children*" (Proverbs 17:6), and Proverbs 13:22 makes it clear that parents should leave an inheritance to their grandchildren.

Inheritances can self destruct

God issues a powerful warning: "*An inheritance quickly gained at the beginning will not be blessed at the end*" (Proverbs 20:21). This represents one of the biggest challenges for the affluent. As the baby-boomer generation passes, unprecedented wealth is cascading down the generations.

Fortunes can tend to self-destruct by destroying the lives of those who inherit them. There is sobering evidence that an inheritance can have a powerful and harmful effect on the recipient. Studies show that the expectation of an inheritance diminishes personal drive, motivation to work and life purpose. In addition, a reason to look forward to the death of a loved one can have a devastating spiritual impact on one's soul.

You can't take it with you but you can send it on ahead.

A good man leaves an inheritance for his children's children, but a sinner's wealth is stored up for the righteous.

Proverbs 13:22

Death isn't your best opportunity to give, it's the end of your opportunity to give. God rewards acts of faith done while we're still living.

Randy Alcorn

----

*Now all the earth is bright and glad
With the fresh morn;
But all my heart is cold, and dark and sad:
Sun of the soul, let me behold
Your dawn!
Come, Jesus, Lord!
O quickly come, according to Your word!*
Christian Friedrich Richter, German theologian, 1676 – 1711

Five keys to ensuring that an inheritance is a blessing

1. Train your heirs: Help them to develop financial wisdom.

2. Design the wealth transfer to develop your heir's character: Consider specifying amounts for education, car purchase, home deposit, business start-up capital or for grandchildren.

3. Evaluate the impact on your heirs: What is the worst that could happen? Do what you can to make sure God's resources are not wasted.

4. Decide when to transfer: Should you transfer now, on the occasion of a future event, or on death?

5. In all your planning, remember that it is a special privilege and responsibility to select the next stewards of the assets entrusted to you.

Day 27

LAWS OF PROSPERITY

Prosperity, like tithing, is one of those topics that causes differences of opinion; and often people on both sides have strong views. I do not regard a focus on prosperity based on the belief that God is going to bestow great riches on oneself to be a healthy focus, although there are Christians who God *has* richly blessed. For me, to place the verses that talk about prosperity under a microscope without the balance of understanding about how we are to use that prosperity is to repeat the same failing that was in the heart and mind of the rich young ruler whose heart was governed by his wealth.

To define prosperity simply in terms of wealth is to deny a balanced approach to everything the Bible has to say about it. Here are seven 'laws' of prosperity that the Bible reveals in its own words:

Prosperity inebriates men, so that they take delights in their own merits.

John Calvin, French Theologian, 1509 – 1564

The law of wisdom

The highest wisdom resides in God's supreme thought and love. God allows us to obtain godly wisdom and He tells us to give this attention. Proverbs 23:4 says, *"Do not wear yourself out to get rich; have the wisdom to show restraint."* How do we obtain wisdom? James 1:5 says, *"If any of you lack wisdom he should ask God, who gives generously to all without finding fault, and it will be given to him."* Proverbs 9:10 and Psalm 111:10 tell us that fear of the Lord is the beginning of wisdom.

> *Blessed are all who fear the Lord, who walk in his ways. You will eat the fruit of your labour; blessings and prosperity will be yours.*
> **Psalm 128:1-2**

Let temporal things serve your use, but the eternal be the object of your desire.

Thomas A Kempis, Catholic monk, 1380 – 1471

The law of priority

Enduring success can be achieved only when we prioritise in accordance with divine instruction – at all levels, including financial matters. We read in Joshua 1:8, *"This Book of the Law shall not depart from your mouth, but you shall meditate in it day and night, that you may observe to do according to all that is written in it. For then you will make your way prosperous, and then you will have good success"* (NKJV).

The law of motive

Meaningful work and living are motivated by unconditional love for others. In Proverbs 16:2 we read, *"All the ways of a man are pure in his own eyes, but the Lord weighs the spirits"* (NKJV). Further on in Proverbs 21:2 it says, *"All the ways of a man seem right to him, but the Lord weighs the heart,"* while Proverbs 27:19 says, *"As water reflects a face, so a man's heart reflects the man."*

The law of generosity

Service and giving create abundance, both for others and ourselves. Matthew 6:21 says, *"For where your treasure is, there your heart will be also."* Proverbs 3:9 tells us to, *"Honour the Lord with your wealth, with the firstfruits of all our crops"* (which is what the tithe is – the first ten per cent); *then your barns will be filled to overflowing, and your vats will brim over with new wine"* (Proverbs 3:10). Proverbs 11:25 says, *"A generous man will prosper; he who refreshes others will himself be refreshed,"* while Proverbs 19:17 counsels, *"He who is kind to the poor lends to the Lord, and He will reward him for what he has done."*

A wealthy Christian man who lost everything in a financial downturn was asked if he ever regretted all he had given to the Lord's work. He replied, "What I gave, I still have. What I kept, I lost."

The law of understanding

To be able to love with God's heart we need to see through His eyes and think His thoughts, for these are the ultimate goals for the truly enlightened spirit. Luke 11:34 says, *"Your eye is the lamp of your body. When your eyes are good, your whole body also is full of light. But when they are bad, your body also is full of darkness."* Paul in Colossians 1:9 says, *"For* this reason, since the day we heard about you, we have not stopped praying about you and asking God to fill you with the knowledge of his will through all spiritual wisdom and understanding." That is a great prayer model and certainly one we should pray for anyone whom we counsel. The Psalmist asks God to, "Show me your ways, O Lord, teach me your paths; guide me in truth and teach me" (Psalm 25:4-5).

The law of preparation

Being responsible with and wisely managing life's resources requires commitment to truly important purpose and careful planning. Luke 16: 11 says, "Therefore if you have not been faithful in the use of worldly wealth, who will entrust the true riches to you?" (NASB). Paul in 1 Corinthians 4:2 says, "Moreover, it is required of stewards, that a man be found faithful," (NKJV) while in 2 Timothy 2:21 Paul says, "If a man cleanses himself from the latter [avoiding worldly and empty chatter], he will be an instrument for noble purposes, made holy, useful to the Master and prepared to do any good work."

The law of preservation

Wise stewardship ensures that money principles, values, and spiritual guidance can be passed from one generation to the next. Psalm 25:21 says, "May integrity and uprightness protect me, because my hope is in you." 1 Thessalonians 5:23 tells us, "May God himself, the God of peace, sanctify you through and through. May your whole spirit, soul and body be kept blameless at the coming of our Lord Jesus Christ."

As we seek prosperity in body, mind, and spirit we will be drawn closer to God and understand more fully His will for our life.

Now he who supplies seed to the sower and bread for food will also supply and increase your store of seed and will enlarge the harvest of your righteousness.

2 Corinthians 9:10

Day 28

FINANCIAL PLANNING

Our goals can only be reached through a vehicle of a plan, in which we must fervently believe, and upon which we must vigorously act. There is no other route to success.

Pablo Picasso, Spanish painter, 1881 – 1973

It is rightly said that failing to plan is planning to fail. I always view God as the ultimate planner, and the Bible is replete with His plans for man. He has set clear goals for man, his redemption and his life on this earth and in eternity. He has provided us with what we need to live and reproduce. God has had a plan for each of us from the beginning.

When President Kennedy announced that America was going to land man on the moon by the end of the 1960s the whole nation was galvanised and motivated by the space race and the desire to achieve that goal. Can you remember watching athletes being interviewed after an Olympic event? While some might announce they are retiring most tell how they wish to return and improve their performance in four years time.

Vision and dreams are powerful motivators for both nations and individuals. Add to the mix instruction and godly wisdom from the Bible and you have all you need to achieve your godly financial goals.

What are the key areas where you should plan? Your response to that question will be personal to you and dependent on your situation and maybe how your thinking has evolved during these studies.

Look at your current situation: monthly income and expenditure

Just about the time you make both ends meet, somebody moves the ends.

Do you have more income than expenditure? If not, then look at your expenditure to see where this can be reduced? What are you spending that could be stopped or reduced? Could you and should you earn more money?

Debt

Is your total debt manageable within your budget? Resolve not to allow your debt to increase one penny more. Cut your cards up if that will help. This is one form of plastic surgery that over time will improve how you feel – and maybe even how you look! Use the snowball strategy – start by repaying the smallest debt first and then when this is repaid roll over the money you pay off this debt to the next smallest debt, and so on. Keep this process in place until each and every debt is repaid including educational loans, car loans, and home mortgages.

Your mortgage – if you move, is it really necessary to increase the mortgage? Perhaps you could reduce the term of the mortgage by two to five years? If the interest rate increases in less than five years could your finances cope with an increase of just two percentage points? Why not start saving that margin to prove that you are in control of your finances?

Some couples go over their budgets very carefully every month; others just go over them.

Sally Poplin

Giving

Is giving a priority for you? Do you give from what is left over or out of your firstfruits? "*Honour the Lord with your wealth, with the firstfruits of all your crops*" (Proverbs 3:9). This is repeated in Exodus 23:19: "*Bring the best of the firstfruits of your soil to the house of the Lord your God.*" Remember that you are never more like Jesus than when you are giving, so be generous. Paul encourages us to give proportionately. You are the steward of all that has been entrusted to you. Remember that a tithe is ten per cent of income and that is certainly proportionate to your income. But remember also that it is not just ten per cent that belongs to God – it all belongs to Him. How much are you going to give to the Lord through your church? Will you give to the poor? Do you have some money from which you could give when a need arises?

Include different areas of giving as lines on your budget, include room for miscellaneous giving. Planning to give develops an attitude of generosity and practically empowers you to be generous.

I sincerely believe that once Christians have been educated in God's plan for their finances, they will find a freedom they had never known before.

Larry Burkett

You've heard of prayer warriors. What about giving warriors? God has entrusted us with so much. Perhaps He is raising up a great army of givers, and He's calling us all to enlist.
Randy Alcorn

Saving

Fluctuating interest rates and stock market falls have historically changed the forward planning of many people. Make sure you have some savings to protect your finances from being knocked off balance by the unexpected, and make a long-term commitment to saving. Perhaps in this way you could serve the Lord full-time sooner rather than later.

Develop the habit of saving even if it is only a few pounds a month

To develop the habit you can use several different methods. For example, some commit income from overtime or bonuses to savings. Others set aside a certain per cent of their regular income each month in a savings account, such as an Individual Savings Account (ISA). Still others use an automatic savings plan or an employee payroll plan.

Here is maxim for saving: if you save a portion of your income as soon as you receive it, you will save more. There are two types of savings: short-term and long-term.

Short term savings

Short-term savings should be readily accessible. They may include interest-earning accounts. These are designed to be used for planned future spending – acquiring or replacing items such as domestic appliances and care and making home repairs. Short-term savings should also be set aside for emergencies – an illness, loss of job, or other interruption of income. Financial advisors recommend you establish the goal of saving the equivalent or three to six months of your income for this emergency fund.

Long-term savings

Long-term savings are intended to fund long-term needs and goals such as retirement income and inheritances. Pensions and retirement accounts fall into this category. Except for extreme financial emergencies, these savings should not be used for any purpose other than the needs for which they were established.

Establishing a maximum amount

When a sprinter breaks the tape at the finish line, he stops running. But many people continue accumulating more and more, even though they have

"For I know the plans I have for you," declares the Lord, "plans to prosper you and not to harm you, plans to give you hope and a future."

Jeremiah 29:11

achieved acceptable savings goals. I believe that each of us should establish a maximum amount we are going to save, and once we have 'finished this race'; we should give away the portion of our income that we were saving. This 'finish line' on accumulation protects us against the dangers of hoarding.

Record your answers to these questions and take the opportunity to write down a plan. Where could you add a little stretch into your planning? Ask God to lead you as you record what you sense are the right steps for you to take with your finances. If you are married, share finances and decisions with your spouse. This is one of those areas where couples can share together as they seek to manage what God has given.

Plans fail for lack of counsel, but with many advisers they succeed.

Proverbs 15:22

Investing

"Steady plodding brings prosperity; hasty speculation brings poverty" (Proverbs 21:5, TLB). The original Hebrew word for 'steady plodding' pictures a person filling a large barrel, one handful at a time. Little by little the barrel is filled to overflowing.

The fundamental principle you need to practice to become a successful investor is to spend less than you earn. Then save the difference over a long period of time.

Examine those various investments that are well suited for "steady plodding". Your home mortgage is paid off after years of steady payments. A stock portfolio is built as it is added to, and a business can increase steadily in value through the years as its potential is developed. Ecclesiastes 5:13-16 warns of avoiding risky investments, yet each year thousands of people lose money in highly speculative and sometimes fraudulent investments. It is important to be patient when investing.

James on the future

Now listen, you who say, "Today or tomorrow we will go to this or that city, spend a year there, carry on business and make money." Why, you do not even know what will happen tomorrow. What is your life? You are a mist that appears for a little while and then vanishes. Instead, you ought to say, "If it is the Lord's will, we will live and do this or that." As it is, you boast and brag. All such boasting is evil" (James 4:13-16).

Day 29

ALL EYES ON ETERNITY

What is eternity? Are you certain that when you die you will go to be with God in eternity? Do we really recognise how short our lives are? There are many millions who have already died and yet everyone who has ever lived is still alive. Thank God that eternity is very, very, long!

The Scripture in Mark 8:36: *"What good is it for a man to gain the whole world, yet forfeit his soul?"* is a question full of insight, but also one that presents us with a challenge.

It draws us to a comparison between believers and the love of the world. We are warned that gaining treasures in this life can be only temporary while there is an inherent danger that the pursuit of wealth can also compromise and endanger our eternal perspective.

To 'gain the world' requires a focus and work attitude that can distract us from our spiritual focus. Sadly, many people permit this to happen as they seek to have what is expected or even seemingly required in life. We live our lives by what the world dictates and forget that Jesus told us that the world and everything in it will pass away. Thus, the world and what it offers acts as a decoy to lead us towards loss rather than gain.

Our time on earth is but a jot compared to our time in eternity.

Setting our sights

Setting our sights on eternity gives us hope and sustains our soul, bringing a certainty that there is life beyond the grave – a life that is sustained by God. In Colossians 3:2-4, Paul tells us to, *"Set your minds on things above, not on earthly things. For you died, and your life is now hidden with Christ in God. When Christ, who is your life, appears, then you also will appear with Him in glory."*.

The Oxford dictionary defines eternity as, 'existing always and unchanging, something that is perpetual or everlasting'. Our hearts and minds should be focussed on living a life that has a godly and eternal understanding. God is the same yesterday, today and forever. Contrast that with the world in which we live. Famous people come and go – one day they are important the next they are but a memory. Economies change, sometimes up, sometimes shaken and down. In the last half of the twentieth century and the first part of the twenty-first materialism has been rampant and society has had much with which to occupy itself – from myriad entertainment options to must-have possessions. Sadly, this is where most people's eyes are focussed. Isaiah 55:8 tells us that, *"my thoughts are not your thoughts, neither are your ways my ways, declares the Lord."* Use your possessions, capabilities and energy knowing that your time here on earth is short. Resist putting off what God has called you to do, for none of us knows when we will draw our last breath.

Our real worth is what will be ours in eternity.

You'll not get to heaven and hear God say you should have given less.

We leave it all behind
We come into this world with nothing and we leave with nothing, or as Job 1:21 puts it, *"we are born naked and we leave naked."* Nothing in this world goes with us as we enter eternity – but we can use what we have now as part of our preparation for eternity. We can focus and apply what the Bible teaches. In 1 Corinthians 6:19 Paul tells the Christians at Corinth that their, *"bodies are a temple of the Holy Spirit, who is in you, whom you have received from God? You are not your own."*

For what will it profit a man if he gains the whole world and loses his own soul?
Mark 8:36, NKJV

Everything will be destroyed
Earthly goods will not last forever – they are destined to be totally annihilated. *"The day of the Lord will come like a thief. The heavens will disappear with a roar; the elements will be destroyed by fire, and the earth and everything in it will be laid bare. Since everything will be destroyed in this way, what kind of people ought you to be? You ought to live holy and godly lives"* (2 Peter 3:10-11). Understanding the temporal nature of our possessions should influence us as we consider how we manage our money and possessions.

Impacting eternity today
What are the choices facing you now? How does an eternal perspective influence your decisions? Martin Luther said that on his calendar there were only two days: 'today' and 'that day.' Maybe we should invest all that we are and have only in *that* day.

God is going to have to take some people to heaven feet first, because they keep trying to hold onto everything they have here on earth.

The greatest use of life is to spend it for something that will outlast it.
William James, Psychologist, 1842 – 1910

Day 30

JUST STRETCHING

How do you feel when you are asked to give? I do not mind sharing that I do not always find myself a cheerful giver. I am far from convinced that giving is a natural activity, even though there have been many occasions when I was really excited about making a gift or responding to an appeal. We have been saved from hell by the death of our Saviour who gave more than we will ever be asked to give. So, feast on the words of your church leaders as they preach on stewardship for they act as a reminder for our hearts to be finely tuned to outwork stewardship.

Time to build the house

About 500 years before the birth of Christ, a group of people responded to trusting God in much the same way as some do today. Haggai tells us of a group of Jews who were released from captivity to return to Jerusalem to rebuild and restore the temple of God. The temple was a sacred place where the glory of God resided and without it there was no place to worship.

Although rebuilding the temple was a huge task, initially there was great enthusiasm. Before beginning the work, the people took the altar of God and restored it to its central place. Even though there were no walls or foundations for the temple, the altar was in place so they gathered to worship God.

After a while, however, the people's enthusiasm began to wane and the building work came to a halt, so God sent Haggai to get them back on schedule. Haggai preached a compelling sermon on their refusal to do what the Lord had told them to do:

"This is what the Lord Almighty says: "These people say, 'The time has not yet come for the Lord's house to be built'" (Haggai 1:2). This was an excuse because they had spent the Lord's money on themselves and wanted to postpone the project. They did not have the time to do what the Lord wanted them to do!

Does that sound familiar today? Finding excuses and putting off the things we know we should do? Our trust and interest is in ourselves. God can wait...and wait. I find this true when it comes to obedience in tithing. Haggai had to give the people of God a strong exhortation by saying, *"Is it time for you yourselves to dwell in your panelled houses, and this temple to lie in ruins?"* (Haggai 1:4). Those people had time to build their own houses but not the house of God – and to make matters worse they were building upmarket houses for themselves!

And do not be conformed to this world, but be transformed by the renewing of your mind, that you may prove what is that good and acceptable and perfect will of God

Romans 12:2

Getting committed

When you accepted Christ as Saviour you stretched out and committed your life to Him, starting on a Christian journey for the remainder of your days on earth before joining Him in eternity.

We all stretch and make commitments – but then we have to take action on that commitment. The 42,360 Jews who were taken from Babylon to Jerusalem were excited in the beginning and their commitment was to rebuild and restore the temple. I believe they really meant to do just that. However, time and self-interest intervened and they excused their lack of action. They were willing to renege on their commitment to God and depend on His provisions while they took care of themselves. Consequently the house of God lay in ruins.

Trust in the Lord forever, for in God the Lord, we have an everlasting rock.

Isaiah 26:4

Many have given their lives to the Lord and were initially excited and planned to do all that God required of them. But time and self intervened and soon self grew larger than their commitment to God. Their commitment to Him remains at a low level, and perhaps the light of their commitment is close to extinction. In Hebrews God said, *"Never will I leave you; never will I forsake you"* (Hebrews 13:5).

Are you just stretching now? Or did you stretch in the past? Or have you given up on something that

Wherever you are in your journey to a more generous life, God wants to take you further!

God called you to do? If so, do not feel condemned or think of yourself as a failure, for God is longing for you to allow Him to place His loving arms around you, protect you and provide all your needs – just so long as you will let Him. His love knows no boundaries.

And finally

I end these devotions with a verse that God gave Rhoda and I after we were baptised. May God bless you and keep you ever in Him.

I waited patiently for the Lord, he turned to me and heard my cry. He lifted me out of the slimy pit, out of the mud and mire; he set my feet on a rock and gave me a firm place to stand.
Psalm 40:1-2

1. THE POWER OF COMPOUND INTEREST

Notwithstanding the desperately low rate of return on savings accounts I have always regarded regular saving as the bedrock of an investment strategy. Save consistently, and maximise the advantage of compound interest. Sometimes referred to as the eighth wonder of the world, regular saving combined with compound interest provides a return that varies based on the amount you save, the interest rate you earn on your savings, your tax position and the length of time you save.

1. The amount

The amount you save will be determined by your level of income, the cost of your standard of living, how much debt you have, your commitment to save and how faithfully you budget. It is our hope that you will be able to increase the amount available for saving as you implement these biblical principles.

2. The interest rate

The second variable is the rate of interest you earn on an investment. The following table demonstrates how an investment of £1,000 grows at various average rates of return.

As you can see, the increase in the rate of return has a remarkable impact on the amount accumulated. A two per cent increase more than doubles the amount over 40 years. However, be wary of risky investments that promise a high return. Usually the higher the rate, the higher the risk. That risk might include fluctuating interest rates. Savings institutions have a tendency to change the terms of accounts and so this type of investment, simple as it is, will require a measure of monitoring.

Interest	Year 5	Year 10	Year 20	Year 30	Year 40
4%	1,221	1,491	2,223	3,313	4,940
6%	1,348	1,819	3,310	6,023	10,957
8%	1,490	2,219	4,927	10,935	24,273
10%	1,645	2,707	7,328	19,837	53,700

The previous table does not take into account the effect of inflation. If inflation were on average three per cent throughout the period the returns, expressed in today's pounds, would look like this:

Interest	Year 5	Year 10	Year 20	Year 30	Year 40
4%	1,053	1,109	1,230	1,365	1,514
6%	1,164	1,353	1,832	2,481	3,359
8%	1,285	1,652	2,728	4,505	7,441
10%	1,419	2,014	4,057	8,172	16,462

3. Time

Time is a factor we cannot control, but the graph that follows may help you visualise the benefits of starting now. If a person faithfully saves £2.74 each day – £1,000 per year – and earns 8 per cent on the savings, at the end of 40 years the savings will grow to almost £290,000 and will be earning £1,207 each month in interest alone! Steady plodding pays. However, if the person waits one year before starting, then saves for 39 years, he or she will accumulate £23,000 less. The message of the illustration is this: Start saving now!

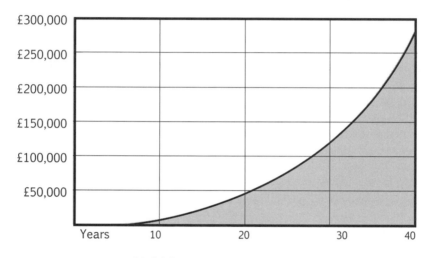

£1,000 invested each year earning 8%

2. HOW TO BUDGET

A budget is useful only if it is used. It should be a plan specifically tailored for managing *your* finances, not someone else's. Some people are more comfortable using a hand-written system, while others prefer using a budget system on a spreadsheet.

To prepare your budget follow these three steps:

Step one – start where you are now

Developing a budget must begin with your current situation. Determine exactly how much household income and expenditure you have. Some people do not know what they are actually earning and spending. For this reason it is essential to keep a record of every penny for a week/month to gain an accurate picture in order to complete an estimated budget.

If your wages or salary are not the same each month (like the income of a commissioned salesperson), make a conservative estimate of your annual income and divide by 12 to establish a working figure for your monthly income.

Then determine which expenses do not necessarily occur each month. Examples are water and gas/electricity, holidays, birthdays and Christmas. Estimate how much these cost for a year and divide that amount by 12 to determine your monthly cost. If you have not kept your bills or receipts, check with your bank and/or credit statement records to see how much you paid. Armed with this information, you can complete the Estimated Weekly/Monthly Budget on page 99. Do not be discouraged. Almost every budget starts out with expenditure in excess of income. But a solution exists.

Step two – the solution is where we want to be

To solve the problem of spending more than your income, you must either increase your income or decrease your expenditure. It is that simple: you need to either earn more or spend less.

Increasing your income

A part-time job, or possibly a project that would involve others in the family are ways of increasing your income. The ever-present danger of increasing income is the tendency for expenses also to rise. To avoid this problem agree to apply any additional income to balancing the budget. Another potential concern is the effect that dedicating more time to work will have on relationships, both within the family and outside in order to earn more money. The 'pain' in order to make the 'gain' needs to be considered.

Reducing your expenditure

When managing my accountacy practice I had many clients who were in seasonal businesses. Some owned holiday lets, others in the fishing tackle and garden centre trades. Whenever I was involved with cash flow planning for seasonal businesses we would always look at the ability of the business to pay an even amount of income to the owner throughout the year. There was no point in

2. HOW TO BUDGET CONTINUED

taking high income during the busy times only to find there was no spare cash when the prime season had past. I also had actor clients and many of them would have other employment in between their acting engagements.

Similarly, if you have fluctuating income, maybe because of commissions, or because you are self-employed, prepare your budget taking a pessimistic viewpoint of your income. Which items of expenditure are absolutely necessary? Which can I do without? Which can I reduce?

You can ask these same questions of your personal budget as you reduce spending. Here are some suggestions to help you evaluate your major expenses.

In order to take a preliminary view of your budget, the crownuk.org website has a range of household costs which look at the key components that comprise the average family budget.

Accommodation

1. Purchase an older house that you can improve yourself. You could also buy a smaller house suitable to your needs today with a design that can be expanded to meet your future needs.

2. Consider apartment living. It can be less expensive and involves fewer responsibilities – garden care, maintenance, etc.

3. If you can do repair and maintenance work such as garden care, maintenance, painting and carpet cleaning, you will save a substantial amount.

4. Which appliances could be switched off? Double glazing and roof insulation reduce energy consumption. Good housekeeping can save 15% of your energy supplies so make sure you don't leave appliances on. Even if you leave the plug in the socket, this uses up energy!

5. Lower the cost of your energy supplies by limiting the use of heating, lights and appliances. Use energy saving light bulbs and A-rated appliances. See energy savingtrust.org.uk for more details.

Food

1. Prepare a menu for the week. Then list the ingredients from the menu and shop according to the list. This will help you plan a nutritionally balanced diet, avoid impulse shopping and eliminate waste.

2. Shop once a week. Each time we go shopping for "some little thing," we always seem to buy "some other little thing" as well.

3. Reduce the ready to eat meals, which have expensive packing added to the cost.

4. Lunches eaten out are often budget breakers. A lunch prepared at home and taken to work will help the budget and the waistline.

Insurance

1. Select insurance based on your need and budget, check the costs at a number of online sites, making comparisons from at least three major insurance companies.

2. Raising the insurance excess feature will substantially reduce premiums.

3. Seek the recommendation of friends for a good insurance agent. A capable agent can save you money. However, make sure you check their rates with those comparable online.

Health

1. Practice preventive medicine. Your body will stay healthier when you get the proper amount of sleep, exercise and have a balanced diet.

2. Practice proper oral hygiene for healthy teeth and to reduce dental bills.

Entertainment and recreation

1. Plan your holidays if you can for the off-peak season and select destinations near home.

2. Rather than expensive entertainment, seek creative alternatives such as picnics or visits to the local parks.

Five budgeting hints

1. Reconcile your bank statement with your bank payments and receipts each month.

2. It is helpful to have a separate savings account where you can deposit the monthly standing order for the bills that do not arise each month. For example, if your annual insurance premium is £480, deposit £40 in this savings account each month. This ensures the money will be available when these payments come due.

3. We are trained to think how we are paid – either weekly or monthly. To better understand the impact of an expense, calculate the yearly cost. For example, if you spend £4 for lunch each working day, multiply by five days a week by 50 weeks a year. That gives an annual cost of over £900. Even a

coffee a day could cost more than £450 a year. Thinking annually provides a different perspective on those small 'inconsequential' costs.

4.   Control your impulse-spending. Impulse-spending ranges from buying expensive items like cars to smaller items such as the latest designer watch. Each time you have the urge to spend for something not planned, post it to an 'impulse list'.

5.   It is wise for husbands and wives to include personal allowances in the budget. Both should be given allowances to spend as they please. Spend within the budget – not a penny more!

Step three – do not stop!

The most common temptation is to stop budgeting. Don't.

Remember, a budget is simply a plan for spending your money. It will not work by itself. Every area of your budget should be regularly reviewed to keep a rein on spending. "*Any enterprise is built by wise planning, becomes strong through common sense, and profits wonderfully by keeping abreast of the facts*" (Proverbs 24:3–4, TLB). There may well be frustrations, but a budget, if properly used, will save you thousands of pounds. It will help you accumulate savings and will help you stay out of debt. More importantly, it will help husbands and wives communicate in an area that is a leading cause of marital conflict.

Commitment

Keep a careful record of all expenditure for 30 days to determine your current situation. After that, plan a budget suited to your income and personal objectives. Put it into effect.

3. ESTIMATED WEEKLY/MONTHLY BUDGET

Gross Income

Gross Income: _____
Salary _____
Benefits _____
Dividends _____
Other income _____

Deduct:
1. Tithe: _____
2. Taxes: _____
3. Other deductions: _____

Net Income A: _____

Living Expenses

4. Housing: _____
Mortgage/rent _____
Insurance _____
Council tax _____
Electricity _____
Gas _____
Water/sewage _____
Telephone/mobile _____
Internet _____
Other _____

5. Food/supermarket: _____

6. Transport: _____
Public transport _____
Car servicing etc. _____
Parking _____
Fuel _____
Insurance _____
MOT/road tax _____
Other: _____

7. Insurance: _____
Life _____
Sickness _____
Other _____

8. Debts: _____
(except mortgage payments)

9. Giving: _____
Sponsored child _____
Generosity _____

10. Entertainment /recreation: _____
Babysitters _____
Holidays _____
Pets _____
Other _____

11. Clothing: _____

12. Medical costs: _____
Dentist _____
Prescriptions _____
Other _____

13. Miscellaneous*: _____
Toiletries/cosmetics* _____
Laundry/cleaning _____
Allowances _____
Subscriptions _____
Birthdays/anniv. _____
Events _____
Christmas presents _____
Conferences _____
Other _____

14. School/child care: _____
Tuition _____
Day care _____
Other _____

15. Savings: _____

16. Investments: _____

Total Expenses B: _____

Income vs. Living Expenses
Net Spendable Income: A: _____
Deduct: Living expenses: B: _____
Surplus or deficit: £: _____

*Where not included in the supermarket account

2,350 VERSES CONTENTS

GOD'S PART

i. God owns everything

a. God owns everything on earth

Genesis 14:19
Genesis 14:22
Exodus 9:29
Exodus 19:5
Deuteronomy 10:14
1 Chronicles 29:11,14-16
Job 41:11
Psalm 24:1
Psalm 50:12
Psalm 82:8
Psalm 89:11
Psalm 95:4-5
Psalm 104:24
1 Corinthians 10:26

1. **Parable illustrating God's ownership**
Matthew 25:14-28

2. **Lord holds all things together**
Hebrews 1:3
Colossians 1:17

b. Specific possessions God owns

1. **Land**
Leviticus 25:23

2. **Gold and silver**
Ezekiel 16:17
Haggai 2:8

3. **Animals**
Psalm 50:10-11

ii. God controls every event

a. Lord controls all events on Earth

1 Chronicles 29:11-12
Psalm 135:6
Proverbs 16:33
Proverbs 20:24
Daniel 2:20-21

» **Lord allows difficult circumstances to occur**
Job 42:11
Isaiah 45:6-7
Lamentations 3:37-38
Amos 3:6

» **Lord uses every circumstances for a good purpose in the life of the godly**
Romans 8:28

» **Example of Lord allowing difficult circumstances for ultimate good**
Genesis 45:5-9

» **A carnal person's perspective of the control of events**
Ecclesiastes 9:11

b. Specific events and items Lord controls

1. **Lord directs people's hearts**
Proverbs 21:1

» **Lord can give godly people favour with others**
Genesis 39:21
Ezra 6:22
Nehemiah 2:8, 18

» **Example of Israelites plundering Egyptians**
Exodus 3:21-22
Exodus 12:35-36

» **Lord makes some people obstinate**
Exodus 14:4
Deuteronomy 2:30

2. **Lord controls the coveting of the heart**
Exodus 34:23-24

» **Lord controls the nations**
Acts 17:26
2 Chronicles 25:7-9
Isaiah 10:5-6

iii. God provides

a. Everything comes from the Lord

1 Chronicles 29:14
Romans 11:36

1. A location called the 'Lord will provide'
Genesis 22:14

2. Lord gives food to all
Psalm 136:25
Psalm 145:15-16

b. Examples of Lord providing

1. In wilderness
Deuteronomy 2:7
Deuteronomy 8:15-16
Nehemiah 9:15
Nehemiah 9:21

2. During Sabbatical year
Leviticus 25:20-22

3. Feeding the multitude
Matthew 14:15-21
Matthew 15:32-38
Matthew 16:8-10
Mark 6:35-44
Mark 8:1-9
Mark 8:18-20
Luke 9:12-17
John 6:5-13

4. At the sea shore
John 21:2-11

c. Lord provides for those who seek and obey Him

Psalm 33:18-19
Psalm 34:9-10
Psalm 81:13,16
Proverbs 10:3
Philippians 4:19
Matthew 6:33
Luke 12:30-31

d. We can be content and anxiety free because He is our provider

(See the *Contentment Scriptures*)

iv. God gives riches and material possessions

a. Everything comes from the Lord

1 Chronicles 29:14
Romans 11:36
1 Timothy 6:17

b. Lord gives riches and material possessions

1 Chronicles 29:12,14-16
Ecclesiastes 5:19
Ecclesiastes 6:1-2
Jeremiah 27:5

1. Examples of Lord giving riches and possessions

» Lord gave children of Israel the promised land
Genesis 35:12
Exodus 6:8
Leviticus 25:38
Deuteronomy 6:10-12
Deuteronomy 8:7-10
Deuteronomy 26:1-3
Joshua 24:13
Nehemiah 9:15
Nehemiah 9:36
Jeremiah 7:5-7

» Other examples
Genesis 24:35
Genesis 26:12-14
Deuteronomy 30:5
1 Samuel 18:14-15
2 Samuel 6:12
2 Chronicles 1:11-12
2 Chronicles 25:6-9
Job 1:9-10
Job 42:10,12
Psalm 105:37
Isaiah 45:3
Jeremiah 27:5-7

GOD'S PART CONTINUED

Ezekiel 16:13,14,17-19
Ezekiel 29:18-19
Hosea 2:8

» **Abraham did not want to give another person credit for his becoming rich**
Genesis 14:22-23

2. **Lord sometimes gives riches after testing and humbling**
Deuteronomy 8:15-18
Psalm 66:10-12

3. **Lord gives possessions to His children even in their sleep**
Psalm 127:2

4. **When Lord gives riches, it is a blessing**
Proverbs 10:22

5. **Lord giving possessions conditioned upon obedience**
(See *Our part Scriptures*)

6. **Lord gives us precisely enough**
2 Samuel 12:7-8

» **According to our ability to handle possessions**
Matthew 25:14-15

c. **Lord causes prosperity**

Genesis 32:9
Genesis 32:12
Genesis 39:2-3
Genesis 39:21-23

1. **Prosperity conditioned upon obedience and seeking the Lord**
(See *Our Part Scriptures*)

2. **Prayers for Lord to bless financially**
Psalm 115:14
Psalm 118:25
3 John 2

d. **Lord gives and takes away possessions**

Job 1:21-22
Job 2:9-10

1. **Lord makes rich and poor**
1 Samuel 2:7
Ecclesiastes 7:14

2. **Lord takes away or withholds possessions when unfaithful, disobedient, or not seeking the Lord**
(See *Our Part Scriptures*)

» **Lord is merciful and will provide a means of restoration**
Judges 2:13-16
Jeremiah 29:14
Jeremiah 32:44
Jeremiah 33:7, 11, 26
Jeremiah 48:47
Jeremiah 49:6
Joel 3:1-2
Zephaniah 2:7
Zephaniah 3:20
Zechariah 8:10-12

3. **Lord takes away wealth of ungodly people and nations**
Proverbs 15:25
Ezekiel 26:12, 14
Zechariah 9:3-4
Zechariah 14:1-2

4. **Lord sometimes transfers wealth from ungodly to godly**
Genesis 31:6-7, 9
Genesis 31:14-16

e. **Lord protects our possessions**

Job 1:9-10
Genesis 31:42

OUR PART

i. Lord gave people authority over the earth

Genesis 1:28
Psalm 8:6
Psalm 115:16
Hebrews 2:6-8

a. Parable illustrating Lord giving people authority over His possessions

Matthew 25:14

ii. Our position is that of a steward

a. Examples of stewards

Genesis 24:2
Genesis 39:4-6
Genesis 39:7-9
1 Corinthians 9:17

iii. Stewards have certain responsibilities

a. Recognise Lord as owner of possessions and transfer ownership to Him

1. Must give ownership of possessions to Lord to be a disciple
Luke 14:33

2. Leaving everything to follow Lord results in blessings
Matthew 19:27-29
Mark 10:28-30
Luke 18:28-30

3. Examples of leaving everything to follow Lord
Mark 1:20
Luke 5:11
Luke 5:27-28

4. Parable illustrating leaving everything to follow Lord
Matthew 13:44-46

b. Be faithful

1 Corinthians 4:2

1. Blessings of faithfulness
Proverbs 28:20
Matthew 24:44-46

» **Blessed with more intimate fellowship with the Lord**
Matthew 25:21

» **Blessed with more responsibility**
Matthew 25:20-23
Luke 12:42-44
Luke 19:12-26

2. Cursed for unfaithfulness
Matthew 24:48-51
Matthew 25:14-30
Luke 12:45-47
Luke 19:12-26

» **Example of unfaithful steward**
Luke 16:1-8

c. Be obedient/seek the Lord

1. Blessings of obedience/seeking the Lord
Deuteronomy 7:12-13
Deuteronomy 15:4-6
Deuteronomy 28:1-14
Deuteronomy 29:9
Deuteronomy 30:9-10
Deuteronomy 30:15-16
Joshua 1:8
1 Kings 2:3
1 Chronicles 22:12-13
1 Chronicles 28:8
Psalm 37:4
Psalm 128:1-2

» **Examples of obedience and blessing**
2 Kings 18:6-7
2 Chronicles 14:7
2 Chronicles 26:5
2 Chronicles 31:20-21
Isaiah 30:22-23

OUR PART CONTINUED

2. Curse of disobedience/not seeking
   the Lord
   Deuteronomy 28:15-18, 33
   Deuteronomy 28:45-48, 63
   Deuteronomy 30:15-18
   Ezra 7:26

» Example of disobedience and
   cursing
   Judges 2:13-14
   2 Chronicles 21:12-14,16,17
   2 Chronicles 24:20
   Nehemiah 9:33-36
   Jeremiah 10:21
   Ezekiel 16:17-19, 39
   Haggai 1:4-11
   Haggai 2:15-17

d. Trust in the Lord, not ourselves or
   possessions

1. Blessings/prosperity for those who
   trust in Lord
   Psalm 112:1,3
   Proverbs 22:4
   Proverbs 28:25

2. Consequences of trusting in
   ourselves or our possessions
   Proverbs 11:28
   Jeremiah 17:5-6
   Jeremiah 48:7
   Jeremiah 49:4-5

iv. Held accountable for our stewardship
   Matthew 25:14, 19
   Luke 16:2
   2 Corinthians 5:9-10
   Revelation 20:11-12

DEBT

i. We are encouraged not to be in debt

Romans 13:8

a. Debt compared to slavery

Proverbs 22:7

1. Commanded not to be slaves of others

1 Corinthians 7:23

b. Examples of hardship of debt

1 Samuel 22:1-2
2 Kings 4:1
Nehemiah 5:1-5
Psalm 109:11
Isaiah 50:1

c. Being debt-free was positive

Jeremiah 15:10

d. Debt was considered a curse

Deuteronomy 28:15, 43-45

e. Being debt-free was considered a blessing

Deuteronomy 15:4-6
Deuteronomy 28:1-2, 12

ii. Debt repayment

a. Godly people repay debts

Proverbs 3:27-28

b. Wicked people do not repay debts

Psalm 37:21

c. Lord can supernaturally provide resources to get out of debt

2 Kings 4:1-7

d. Forgiveness of debts every seventh year – a law for Old Testament believers

Deuteronomy 15:1-11
Deuteronomy 31:10-11
Nehemiah 10:31

e. Miscellaneous example of debt repayment

Philemon 18-19

iii. Indebtedness used as examples in teaching

a. Teaching of Jesus Christ

Matthew 18:21-35
Luke 7:40-43

b. Teaching of Paul

Colossians 2:14

iv. Cosigning (surety/ striking hands)

a. Cosigning discouraged

Proverbs 17:18
Proverbs 20:16
Proverbs 27:13

b. Cosigning dangerous

Proverbs 11:15
Proverbs 22:26-27

c. Cosigning deliverance

Proverbs 6:1-5

COUNSEL

i. Counsel encouraged

Proverbs 1:5
Proverbs 1:25
Proverbs 1:30
Proverbs 12:15
Proverbs 13:10
Proverbs 19:20
Proverbs 20:18
Proverbs 27:9
Ecclesiastes 4:13
Luke 13:31

a. Many counsellors encouraged

Proverbs 11:14
Proverbs 15:22
Proverbs 24:5-6

1. Additional people increase productivity
Leviticus 26:8
Ecclesiastes 4:9-12

b. Examples of giving/following counsel

Exodus 18:14-24
1 Kings 1:11-12
Job 29:21-23

c. Example of not giving/following counsel

2 Chronicles 25:14-16

ii. Sources of counsel

a. The Lord

Job 12:13
Psalm 16:7
Psalm 25:12
Psalm 32:8
Psalm 33:10-11
Psalm 73:24
Proverbs 19:21
Isaiah 9:6
Isaiah 11:2
Isaiah 28:29
Jeremiah 32:18-19

1. Consequences of not seeking Lord's counsel
1 Chronicles 10:13-14
Joshua 9:14-15
Psalm 106:13-15
Psalm 107:10-12

2. The Lord controls the counsel of people
2 Samuel 15:31, 33-34
2 Samuel 16:20, 23
2 Samuel 17:6-23

b. Scripture

Psalm 119:24

c. Godly people

1. Mother and father
Proverbs 1:8-9
Proverbs 6:20-22
Proverbs 23:22

» **Example of godly father's counsel**
1 Kings 2:1-4

2. Those gifted with wisdom
2 Chronicles 9:23
Proverbs 13:20
1 Corinthians 12:8

3. Experienced people
1 Kings 12:6-8
2 Chronicles 10:6-8

iii. Counsel to be avoided

a. The wicked

Job 21:14-16
Psalm 1:1
Proverbs 12:5

1. Example of evil counsel
Ezra 4:4-5
Nahum 1:11

2. Idolatrous people
Deuteronomy 32:28
Isaiah 41:28-29

b. Inexperienced

    1 Kings 12:8-10, 13-14

    2 Chronicles 10:8-10, 13-14

iv. Blessings and curses

a. Blessings and benefits of seeking
   counsel

1. Success
   Proverbs 11:14
   Proverbs 15:22
   Proverbs 24:6

2. Direction and guidance
   Psalm 32:8
   Psalm 73:24
   Proverbs 6:20-22

3. Wisdom
   Proverbs 13:10
   Proverbs 19:20

4. Joy in giving counsel
   Proverbs 12:20

b. Curses/consequences of not
   seeking counsel or seeking wicked
   counsel

1. Death
   1 Chronicles 10:13,14
   2 Chronicles 22:3-5
   2 Chronicles 25:16
   Proverbs 1:24-32

2. Strife
   Proverbs 13:10

3. Plans frustrated
   Proverbs 15:22

4. Failure
   Proverbs 11:14

5. Miscellaneous curses and
   consequences
   Joshua 9:14-15
   Psalm 106:13-15
   Psalm 107:10-12

HONESTY

i. People are dishonest

a. Human heart is dishonest

Genesis 8:21
Jeremiah 17:9
Matthew 15:19
Mark 7:21-22

b. People practice relative honesty

Judges 17:6

c. Examples of dishonest people

Genesis 31:7
Joshua 7:11, 20-21
1 Samuel 8:3
1 Kings 21:19
Psalm 58:3
Isaiah 1:23
Isaiah 56:11
Jeremiah 6:13
Jeremiah 7:9, 11
Ezekiel 22:27, 29
Hosea 4:1-2
Hosea 5:10
Hosea 7:1
Hosea 12:7
Micah 6:10-12
John 12:4-6
John 18:40
Acts 5:1-10
Titus 1:12
Revelation 9:20-21

1. Parable using dishonesty as illustration

Luke 16:1-8

d. Dishonesty concealed by religion

Jeremiah 7:9-11
Matthew 21:12-13
Matthew 23:25
Mark 11:15-17
Luke 11:39
Luke 19:45-46
Titus 1:10-11

ii. God demands absolute honesty

a. The Lord is truth, satan a liar

1. The Lord is truth

John 1:14
John 14:6
John 16:13
1 John 5:7

2. Satan is a liar

John 8:44

b. Under Old Testament law

Exodus 20:15
Leviticus 19:11-13
Leviticus 19:35-36
Leviticus 25:14-17
Deuteronomy 5:19
Deuteronomy 19:14
Deuteronomy 25:13-16

c. As a general biblical principle

Psalm 34:13
Psalm 51:6
Psalm 62:10
Proverbs 3:3
Proverbs 4:24
Proverbs 6:12
Proverbs 6:16, 19
Proverbs 11:1
Proverbs 12:22
Proverbs 13:5
Proverbs 14:5
Proverbs 14:25
Proverbs 17:7
Proverbs 16:11
Proverbs 20:10
Proverbs 20:23
Proverbs 22:22-23
Proverbs 22:28
Proverbs 23:10
Proverbs 23:23
Proverbs 28:24
Lamentations 3:35-36
Zechariah 8:16-17

Luke 3:12-14
Romans 2:21-22
Corinthians 6:7-10
Ephesians 4:25
Ephesians 6:14
Colossians 3:9
1 Thessalonians 5:22
1 Timothy 1:9-10
Titus 2:9-10
1 Peter 1:15-16
1 Peter 4:15

d. Required of leaders

1. Government
Exodus 18:21-22
Proverbs 20:28
Proverbs 28:16
Ezekiel 45:9-10

2. Church
1 Timothy 3:8
Titus 1:7
1 Peter 5:1-2

e. Honesty required in giving

Malachi 1:13-14

1. Not giving properly considered robbery
Malachi 3:8-9

f. Honesty more valuable than riches

Proverbs 19:1
Proverbs 19:22
Proverbs 28:12

g. Examples of honest people

Numbers 16:15
1 Samuel 12:3-5
Job 31:5, 8
Daniel 6:4
Daniel 6:22
Zephaniah 3:13

1. Example of testing people for honesty
Genesis 42:11, 18-20
Genesis 42:31-34

h. Godly people hate dishonesty

Proverbs 13:5

iii. Why does God demand absolute honesty?

a. We cannot be dishonest and love God

Proverbs 14:2

b. We cannot be dishonest and love our neighbour

Proverbs 26:28
Romans 13:9-10

c. Honesty creates credibility for evangelism

Philippians 2:15

d. Honesty helps direct our lives

Proverbs 4:24-26

e. Even the smallest dishonesty is devastating

Luke 16:10

iv. How can we escape the temptation to be dishonest?

a. By the Lord's grace and power

Psalm 119:36
Proverbs 30:7-8
Galatians 5:16-17

HONESTY CONTINUED

b. **By practicing the golden rule**

Matthew 7:12
Philippians 2:4

c. **By a healthy fear of the Lord**

Proverbs 16:6

d. **Isolating ourselves from the dishonest**

Psalm 26:4
Psalm 40:4
Psalm 101:6-7
Proverbs 1:10-16
Proverbs 29:24
1 Corinthians 5:9-11
1 Corinthians 15:33

e. **By giving**

Ephesians 4:28

f. **By establishing a system of accountability**

Genesis 30:31-33

v. What do we do when we have acted dishonesty?

a. **Restore our fellowship with the Lord**

Leviticus 5:5-6
Leviticus 6:1-5, 7
1 John 1:9

b. **Restore our fellowship with the harmed person**

Proverbs 28:13
James 5:16

c. **Restore any stolen property**

Exodus 22:1-4
Exodus 22:7-9
Exodus 22:14

Leviticus 6:1-5
Numbers 5:5-8
2 Samuel 12:5-6
Proverbs 6:30-31
Ezekiel 33:14-16
Luke 19:8

vi. Blessings and curses

a. **Blessings promised for the honest**

1. **Blessing of a more intimate relationship with the Lord**
Psalm 15:1-4
Psalm 24:3-4
Psalm 145:18
Proverbs 3:3-4
Proverbs 3:32
Proverbs 12:22
Jeremiah 22:15-17

2. **Blessing of protection**
Proverbs 2:7
Proverbs 10:9

3. **Blessing of provision**
Isaiah 33:15-16

4. **Blessing on the family**
Proverbs 20:7

5 **Blessing of happiness**
Proverbs 10:2

6. **Blessing of life**
Deuteronomy 25:13-15
Psalm 34:12-13
Proverbs 12:19
Ezekiel 33:14-16

7. **Blessing of the respect of people**
Proverbs 3:3-4

8. **Blessing of prosperity**
Proverbs 15:6

9. **Blessing for leaders**
Proverbs 28:16

b. **Curses reserved for the dishonest**

1. **Curse of being hated/separated from God**
   Deuteronomy 25:13-16
   Psalm 5:6
   Proverbs 3:32
   Proverbs 6:16, 19
   Proverbs 12:22
   Proverbs 19:9
   Isaiah 57:17
   Isaiah 59:2-4

2. **Curse of punishment/judgement**
   Deuteronomy 27:17
   Psalm 63:11
   Proverbs 12-15
   Proverbs 19:5
   Proverbs 20:17
   Isaiah 57:17
   Jeremiah 5:27-29
   Jeremiah 9:3-9
   Ezekiel 22:13-15
   Ezekiel 22:27-31
   Hosea 5:10
   Amos 8:4-10
   Micah 6:10-16
   Matthew 21:12-13
   Luke 19:45-46

3. **Curse of death/destruction**
   Joshua 7:11, 15, 25
   Psalm 5:6
   Psalm 52:3-5
   Proverbs 1:19
   Proverbs 6:12, 15
   Proverbs 12:19
   Proverbs 21:6
   Proverbs 22:8
   Proverbs 22:22-23
   Jeremiah 22:17-19
   Ezekiel 18:10-13, 18
   Acts 5:1-10

4. **Curse on family**
   Proverbs 15:27
   Jeremiah 8:10
   Micah 2:1-3

5. **Curse on possessions**
   Genesis 31:7, 9
   Proverbs 10:2

Proverbs 13:11
Jeremiah 6:12-13
Jeremiah 17:11
Micah 4:13

6. **Curse of pride**
   Proverbs 22:8

7. **Curse on a leader's subordinates**
   Proverbs 29:12

8. **Curse in eternity**
   Revelation 21:8
   Revelation 21:27
   Revelation 22:15

9. **Curses in general**
   Deuteronomy 27:17
   Proverbs 20:17
   Nahum 3:1

c. **People's view of God not punishing dishonesty**
   Job 24:1-2, 12

vii. Bribes

a. **People bribe**

1. **Bribes are effective**
   Proverbs 17:8
   Proverbs 21:14

2. **Wicked people bribe**
   Psalm 26:9-10
   Proverbs 17:23

3. **Examples of those who bribed**
   1 Samuel 8:3
   Isaiah 1:23
   Micah 7:3
   Matthew 28:11-15
   Acts 24:25-26

b. Commanded not to participate in a bribe

Exodus 23:8
Deuteronomy 16:19

1. Bribes corrupt
Ecclesiastes 7:7

2. Lord example of not taking bribe
Deuteronomy 10:17

3. Leaders cannot take bribes
2 Chronicles 19:7
Proverbs 29:4

4. Examples of those who did not take bribes
1 Samuel 12:3-5
Job 6:22

c. Blessings and curses

1. Those who bribe are curses
Deuteronomy 27:25
Isaiah 5:23
Ezekiel 22:12-15
Amos 5:11-12
Micah 3:11-12

2. Those who do not bribe are blessed
Psalm 15:1, 5
Proverbs 15:27
Isaiah 33:15-1

GIVING

i. Tests of giving

a. Test of faith

James 2:14-17

b. Test of love of God abiding in us

1 John 3:17

c. Test of loving our neighbour

2 Corinthians 8:8

1. Example of Good Samaritan
Luke 10:33-35

d. Test of lordship

Matthew 19:21-22
Mark 10:21-22
Luke 18:22-23

ii. Attitudes in giving

a. God's attitude

John 3:16
1 John 4:16
James 1:17

b. Our attitude

1. What is the proper attitude?

» In love
1 Corinthians 13:3

» Cheerful
2 Corinthians 9:7

2. How do we give with love?

» Give to the Lord as an expression of love and worship
Exodus 25:2
Exodus 30:12-14
Exodus 35:5
Exodus 35:21-29
Leviticus 7:14
Numbers 18:8-24
1 Chronicles 18:11
2 Chronicles 32:23

2 Samuel 8:11
Psalm 50:14
Psalm 66:13
Psalm 68:29
Psalm 76:11
Ezekiel 20:40
Micah 4:13

» All we possess is from the Lord and we are giving back to Him
1 Chronicles 29:14-16

» Example of the Christ Child
Matthew 2:1

» Example of not giving to the Lord
Isaiah 43:23-24

3. Give cheerfully by submitting to the Lord/offer willingly
1 Chronicles 29:5-9
1 Chronicles 29:14-17
2 Corinthians 8:1-5

4. Attitude more important than the amount given
Matthew 23:23
Luke 11:42
Luke 18:10-14

» Giving with the proper attitude/ Lord accepting gift
Genesis 4:4
Hebrews 11:4
Philippians 4:18

» Giving with wrong attitude/Lord rejecting gift
Genesis 4:3-5
Amos 4:4-6
Amos 5:22, 24
Amos 5:25-27
Malachi 2:13-14

» Lying to Holy Spirit
Acts 5:1-10

» To justify sin
Proverbs 7:14

iii. Advantages of giving

a. Benefits for the giver

Acts 20:35

GIVING CONTINUED

1. **Increase in intimacy with Lord**
   Matthew 6:21
   Luke 12:34

2. **Increase in heaven**
   Matthew 6:20
   Matthew 19:21
   Luke 12:33
   Luke 18:22
   Philippians 4:17
   1Timothy 6:17-19

3. **Increase on earth**
   Deuteronomy 14:28-29
   2 Chronicles 31:10
   Proverbs 3:9-10
   Proverbs 11:24-25
   Ecclesiastes 11:1
   Luke 6:38
   2 Corinthians 9:6-11
   Philippians 4:19

   » **Challenge to test Lord for material increase**
   Malachi 3:10

4. **Increase in blessings**
   Ezekiel 44:30
   Luke 7:2-5
   Acts 9:36-37, 40
   Acts 10:1-4, 31

iv. Amount to give

a. **Tithe**

1. **Before the law**
   Genesis 14:20
   Genesis 28:20-22

2. **Under the law**
   Leviticus 27:30-32

   » **Not tithing considered robbing God**
   Malachi 3:8-9

   » **Tithe eaten in presence of Lord**
   Deuteronomy 14:22-26

   » **Tithe given to support Levites and poor**
   Numbers 18:21-24
   Deuteronomy 14:28-29

   Deuteronomy 26:12
   2 Chronicles 31:4-12
   Nehemiah 10:37-38
   Nehemiah 13:10-11

   » **Levites were to tithe from their tithe**
   Numbers 18:26

3. **Tithe in the New Testament**

   » **Jesus condemns the Pharisees (see ii 4)**

   » **The superiority of priesthood of Melchizedek**
   Hebrews 7:1-2, 4-9

4. **Storehouse tithe**
   2 Chronicles 31:11-12
   Nehemiah 10:38
   Nehemiah 12:44
   Nehemiah 13:12

b. **Offerings**
   (See sections iv and viii)

c. **Proportionate giving**
   (as God prospers)

   Deuteronomy 16:10, 16
   1 Corinthians 16:2

1. **Examples of proportionate giving**
   Ezra 2:69
   Acts 11:29

2. **Acceptable amount given in proportion to one's means**
   2 Corinthians 8:12

d. **Sacrificial giving**

   Mark 12:41-44
   Luke 21:1-4
   2 Corinthians 8:1-4

1. **Do not give something that costs you nothing**
   2 Samuel 24:21-24
   1 Chronicles 21:22-24

2. **Cursed when giving something stolen or blemished**
   Malachi 1:6-14

v. Approach to giving

a. **Pattern for giving**

1. **Priority**
   Exodus 23:10-11
   Exodus 34:19
   Exodus 34:26
   Leviticus 2:12
   Numbers 28:26
   Deuteronomy 26:1-2
   Proverbs 3:9

2. **Promptly**
   Exodus 22:29
   Deuteronomy 23:21
   Ecclesiastes 5:4

3. **Premeditated**
   2 Corinthians 9:7

4. **Periodic**
   1 Corinthians 16:2

5. **Personal**
   Exodus 34:20
   Deuteronomy 16:17
   Ezekiel 45:16
   Acts 11:29
   1 Corinthians 16:2

6. **Private deposit**
   1 Corinthians 16:2

7. **Pride less**
   Matthew 6:1-4

8. **Prompted heart**
   Exodus 25:2
   Exodus 35:5
   Exodus 35:21-29
   2 Kings 12:4

b. **Policies for giving**

1. **Administration and accountability**
   1 Chronicles 26:20
   1 Chronicles 26:26
   2 Chronicles 31:14-15
   Nehemiah 12:44
   Nehemiah 13:13
   2 Corinthians 8:18-21
   Acts 11:30
   1 Corinthians 16:3-4

   » **Examples of not requiring accountability**
   2 Kings 12:15
   2 Kings 22:7

c. **Places to give**

1. **Family**
   1 Timothy 5:8

   » **Parents**
   Matthew 15:4-6
   Mark 7:9-13

   » **Widows**
   1 Timothy 5:4
   1 Timothy 5:16

   » **Example of giving to family**
   Genesis 45:11
   Genesis 47:12

2. **Ministry**
   Levitical priests (also see iv)
   Leviticus 2:3
   Leviticus 7:14
   Leviticus 7:32-34
   Leviticus 10:12-14
   Numbers 5:8-10
   Numbers 18:8-19
   Numbers 31:28-30
   Deuteronomy 18:3-4
   Deuteronomy 25:4
   Nehemiah 10:35-36
   Nehemiah 12:47
   Ezekiel 44:29-30

   » **New Testament workers**
   Matthew 10:9-10
   Mark 6:8
   Luke 9:1-3

Luke 10:1, 4-7
Galatians 6:6
1 Timothy 5:17-18
Titus 3:13
3 John 1:5-8

» **Jesus supported by gifts during his earthly ministry**
Luke 8:3

» **Christian workers who did not exercise their right to be supported**
1 Corinthians 9:6-15
1 Corinthians 9:17-18
2 Corinthians 11:7-9
2 Corinthians 12:14-18
1 Thessalonians 2:5, 9
2 Thessalonians 3:8-9

» **Christian workers must not minister with evil financial intentions**
1 Peter 5:1-2

» **Many attempt to get money by appearing to be religious**
2 Corinthians 2:17
Titus 1:10-11
2 Peter 2:1, 3

» **Disciples urged to prepare**
Luke 22:35-36

d. **The sanctuary/temple**

» **The building of the sanctuary**
Exodus 25:3-8

» **Gave more than enough**
Exodus 36:3-7

» **The building of the temple**
1 Chronicles 29:2-8

» **The temple cost a great deal**
1 Kings 5:17

» **The repair of the temple**
2 Kings 12:4-11
2 Kings 22:4-6
2 Chronicles 24:4-13
2 Chronicles 34:8-11

1. **The rebuilding of the temple**
Ezra 2:68-69
Ezra 6:4
Ezra 6:8

2. **Maintenance of the temple**
Nehemiah 10:30, 39

3. **Miscellaneous categories**

» **Those who ask for a gift**
Matthew 5:42
Luke 6:30

» **All people, especially believers**
Galatians 6:10
Romans 12:10, 13

» **Enemies**
Proverbs 25:21-22
Romans 12:20

» **Do not give to a murderer**
Proverbs 28:17

vi. Giving to the poor

a. **God's commands and perspective of giving to the poor**

Deuteronomy 15:11
Proverbs 14:31
Proverbs 19:17
Isaiah 58:6-10
Ezekiel 16:49

1. **Old Testament provisions for the poor**

» **Laws of harvesting and gleaning**
Exodus 23:10-11
Leviticus 19:9-10
Leviticus 23:22
Deuteronomy 24:19-21

» **Forgiveness of debts (see Debt section)**

» **Unlimited liability of meeting needs**
Deuteronomy 15:7-10

» **Celebration of Purim**
Ester 9:22

» **Tithe to poor (see iv. a)**

» **Year of Jubilee**
Leviticus 25:10

» **Examples of giving to the poor**
Job 29:12-16
Job 31:16-23

» **Righteous leader**
Psalm 72:4, 12-13

» **Excellent wife**
Proverbs 31:10, 20

2. **New Testament**

» **John the Baptist**
Luke 3:10-11

» **Jesus Christ identifies with poor**
Matthew 25:31-45

» **Jesus models giving to the poor**
John 13:27-29

» **Formerly dishonest to give to the poor**
Ephesians 4:28

» **Other examples**
Acts 2:44-45
Acts 11:28-30
Acts 20:35
Romans 15:26-27
Galatians 2:10

b. **Blessings and curses**

1. **Blessings of giving to the poor**

» **Blessing of knowing the Lord**
Jeremiah 22:16

» **Blessing of life**
Ezekiel 18:7, 9, 16-17

» **Blessing on family**
Psalm 112:2, 9

» **Blessing of needs met**
Proverbs 28:27

» **Blessing of health**
Psalm 41:1-3

» **Blessing of prayers answered and guidance**
Isaiah 58:6-11

» **Blessing of delivery and protection**
Psalm 41:1-2

» **Blessing of honour**
Psalm 112:9

» **Blessing on work and of wealth**
Deuteronomy 15:10
Deuteronomy 24:19

Psalm 72:4, 12-15
Psalm 112:3, 9
Proverbs 19:17
Proverbs 28:8
Daniel 4:27

» **Blessing of spiritual fruitfulness**
Titus 3:13-14

» **Blessings in general**
Proverbs 22:9

» **Blessings of happiness**
Proverbs 14:21

2. **Curses for those who do not give to the poor**

» **Curse of unanswered prayer**
Proverbs 21:13

» **Curse of poverty**
Proverbs 22:16

» **Cursed in general**
Proverbs 28:27

c. **Miscellaneous issues in giving to the poor**

1. **Attitude of compassion**
Job 30:25

2. **Investigate the needs of the poor**
Job 29:16

3. **Godly accused of not giving to the poor**
Job 22:5, 7, 9

4. **Example of giving glory to God instead of giving to the poor**
Matthew 26:6-13
Mark 14:3-7
John 12:3-8

5. **Care of widows required**
Acts 6:1-3
James 1:27

6. **Results of proper ownership perspective: no poor**
Acts 4:32-33

7. **There were provisions for the poor to give less**
Leviticus 5:7, 11
Leviticus 12:6, 8

Leviticus 14:21-22
Leviticus 14:30-32
Leviticus 27:8

» **Jesus' parents were in this category**
Luke 2:22-24

» **During census rich and poor gave same amount**
Exodus 30:12-15

8. **Giving to the poor can be evidence of salvation**
Luke 19:8-9

vii. Miscellaneous examples of giving (not to the Lord)

Genesis 24:22, 53
Genesis 43:11-12, 15
2 Chronicles 9:8-9
2 Chronicles 9:12
2 Chronicles 31:23
2 Chronicles 32:23
2 Chronicles 35:7-9
Ezra 1:4, 6
Nehemiah 7:70-72
Esther 2:18
Psalm 72:10
Jeremiah 40:5

a. **To appease others**

Genesis 32:13, 20
Genesis 33:8-11
Proverbs 21:14

b. **To influence others**

Genesis 34:11-12

c. **To seek wisdom**

2 Chronicles 9:23-24
1 Kings 10:10

d. **Wicked celebrate the death of the godly**

Revelation 11:10

viii. Miscellaneous giving issues

a. **Location to give**

Exodus 23:19
Exodus 34:26
Deuteronomy 12:6
Deuteronomy 12:11
Deuteronomy 12:17-18

b. **We may have no money to give, but we can give Christ**

Acts 3:2-6

c. **Generous person will have many requests to give**

Proverbs 19:6

d. **Giving can be affected by covetousness**

2 Corinthians 9:5

e. **Giving results in thanksgiving to God**

2 Corinthians 9:12

f. **Do not give before attempting reconciliation**

Matthew 5:23-24

g. **Scripture encourages us to give**

Nahum 1:15
Hebrews 13:16

h. **Giving can be a testimony**

Matthew 8:4
Mark 1:44
Luke 5:14

i. **Example of giving to an nation**

Acts 24:17

j. Things better than a sacrifice

1. Love of God and neighbour
   Mark 12:33

2. Loyalty to and knowledge of God
   Hosea 6:6

3. Obedience
   1 Samuel 15:22
   Isaiah 1:11

4. Righteousness/justice
   Proverbs 21:3

k. Offerings

1. Compulsory
   Ezekiel 46:11-15

2. Voluntary
   Ezekiel 46:12

3. Examples of offerings
   1 Kings 8:62-64
   Ezra 1:2, 4, 6
   Ezra 7:15-18, 20-22

l. If your spiritual gift is giving, exercise it

Romans 12:6-8

m. Give to meet needs

Exodus 16:18
2 Corinthians 8:13-15

WORK

i. Biblical perspective of work

a. Work necessary

1. Lord himself is a worker
Genesis 2:2-3
Genesis 2:8
John 5:17

2. **Required in Old Testament**
Exodus 20:9
Exodus 23:12
Exodus 34:21
Deuteronomy 5:13

3. **Required in New Testament**
Ephesians 4:28
2 Thessalonians 3:8-12

4. **Work expected**
Psalm 104:23

b. The requirement to work not a consequence of sin

1. **Lord commanded people to work before the fall**
Genesis 2:15

2. **Lord commanded people to work after the fall, but work more difficult**
Genesis 3:17-19, 23
Genesis 5:29

c. All honest work honourable

1. **Examples of godly peoples' vocations**

» **Farmer**
Genesis 2:15
Genesis 4:2
Genesis 9:20
Genesis 46:32
Genesis 47:3
Amos 7:14

» **Domestic worker**
Genesis 39:4

» **Government workers and leaders**
Genesis 41:41
Genesis 45:26
Nehemiah 4:14
Psalm 105:21
Daniel 2:48
Daniel 6:1-2
Daniel 8:27
Acts 8:27

» **Fishermen**
Matthew 4:18
Mark 1:16
Mark 1:20

» **Building trades**
Matthew 13:55
Mark 6:3
Acts 18:2-3

» **Tax collectors**
Mark 2:14
Luke 5:27
Luke 19:2

» **Retailer**
Acts 16:14

d. Work as unto the Lord

1 Corinthians 10:31
Ephesians 6:5-9
Colossians 3:17
Colossians 3:23-24

1. **Some people view work as a useless vanity**
Ecclesiastes 1:3
Ecclesiastes 2:4-5, 10-11
Ecclesiastes 2:18-24
Ecclesiastes 3:9-10, 13
Ecclesiastes 4:4-6
Ecclesiastes 5:18-19
Ecclesiastes 6:7

e. Our work should be the work God intends for us

1 Samuel 2:28
Psalm 90:17
John 4:34
John 6:27
Acts 13:36

1 Corinthians 3:13-15
Ephesians 2:10

1. **Work that will glorify the Lord**
John 17:4

2. **Productive to know precise work Lord has for us**
John 21:3-11

3. **Work is useless apart from the Lord**
Psalm 127:1
Proverbs 16:3

» **There must be no selfish ambition in work**
Romans 2:6, 8
2 Corinthians 5:9-10
James 3:14-16

» **Do not desire greatness for self**
Jeremiah 45:5

4. **Strong, courageous and do not procrastinate**
Joshua 1:6-7
1 Chronicles 22:10, 13, 16
1 Chronicles 28:20
2 Chronicles 15:7
Haggai 2:4

» **We will encounter difficulties when doing work Lord has for us**
Ezra 4:4-5
Nehemiah 4:15-22
Nehemiah 6:3, 9

f. **Work hard**

Proverbs 12:27
Ecclesiastes 9:10
Ecclesiastes 11:6

1. **Examples of hard workers**
Genesis 31:38-40
Nehemiah 2:18
Nehemiah 4:6
Acts 20:34
1 Corinthians 4:11-12
2 Corinthians 11:27
Colossians 1:29
1 Thessalonians 2:9
2 Thessalonians 3:8

2. **Hunger motivates us to work**
Proverbs 16:26

3. **Hard workers should be paid first**
2 Timothy 2:6

4. **Benefits of work/hard work**

» **Needs met**
Proverbs 12:11
Proverbs 27:18
Proverbs 28:19

» **Profit and wealth**
Proverbs 10:4-5
Proverbs 13:11
Proverbs 14:23
Proverbs 21:5

» **Satisfied soul**
Proverbs 13:4

» **Leadership**
Proverbs 12:24

» **Restful sleep**
Ecclesiastes 5:12

» **Happiness**
Psalm 128:1-2

5. **Do not overwork**
Psalm 127:2

» **Do not overwork to get rich**
Proverbs 23:4

6. **Laziness condemned**
Proverbs 6:6-8
Proverbs 10:5
Proverbs 10:26
Proverbs 12:27
Proverbs 15:19
Proverbs 18:9
Proverbs 19:24
Proverbs 22:13
Proverbs 26:13-16

7. **Consequences of laziness**

» **Hunger**
Proverbs 19:15
Proverbs 20:4

» **Poverty**
Proverbs 6:9-11
Proverbs 10:4
Proverbs 14:23
Proverbs 20:13
Proverbs 23:21
Proverbs 24:30-34
Ecclesiastes 10:18

» **Death**
Proverbs 21:25

» **Starved soul**
Proverbs 13:4

» **Forced labour**
Proverbs 12:24

g. **Take time from work for rest and worship**

1. **Sabbath**

» **Lord established Sabbath**
Genesis 2:2-3
Exodus 20:11
Exodus 31:17
Hebrews 4:4, 10

» **Sabbath required in Old Testament**
Exodus 12:16
Exodus 20:9-10
Exodus 23:12
Exodus 34:21
Exodus 35:2
Leviticus 23:3
Deuteronomy 5:13-14
Nehemiah 10:31
Jeremiah 17:21-22, 24

» **Penalty for not serving Sabbath**
Exodus 31:15
Numbers 15:32-35
Nehemiah 13:15-18
Jeremiah 7:27

2. **Sabbatical year**
Exodus 23:10-11
Leviticus 25:1-5
Nehemiah 10:31

» **Consequences of not observing sabbatical year**
Leviticus 26:34
Leviticus 26:43

3. **Year of Jubilee**
Leviticus 25:11

4. **Religious holidays in Old Testament**

» **Passover**
Numbers 28:18
Numbers 28:25
Deuteronomy 16:8

» **Day of Atonement**
Leviticus 16:29
Leviticus 23:27-31

» **Feast of Unleavened Bread**
Leviticus 23:7-8

» **Feast of Booths**
Leviticus 23:34-36
Numbers 29:12, 35

» **Various religious festivals**
Leviticus 23:21
Leviticus 23:24-25
Numbers 28:26
Numbers 29:1
Numbers 29:7

ii. God's part in work

a. **God gives job skills**

Exodus 28:3
Exodus 31:1-3
Exodus 31:6
Exodus 35:30-35
Exodus 36:1-2
1 Chronicles 22:12
2 Chronicles 1:11-12
2 Chronicles 9:23
Ecclesiastes 2:26
Daniel 1:17
Daniel 2:21, 23

b. **God gives success**

Genesis 39:2-3
Ruth 2:12

1 Chronicles 22:11
Nehemiah 2:18, 20
Nehemiah 4:15, 19-20
Nehemiah 6:15-16
John 3:27

c. God ultimately controls promotion

1 Chronicles 29:12
2 Chronicles 9:8
Psalm 75:6-7
Daniel 2:37-38
Daniel 5:21

d. God can motivate people to work

Haggai 1:14

iii. Employer and employee responsibilities

a. Employer responsibilities

1. Pay a fair wage
Jeremiah 22:13
Malachi 3:5

» Example of negotiating for a fair wage
Genesis 29:15
Genesis 30:28

» Punishment for those not paying fair wage
James 5:1, 3-4

» Parable with illustration of paying fair wage
Matthew 20:1-16

2. Pay employee promptly
Leviticus 19:13
Deuteronomy 24:14-15

3. Be just and fair
Colossians 4:1

» Do not threaten, rather serve employee
Ephesians 6:7-9

4. Listen to employee complaints
Job 31:13-15

5. Give employee adequate rest or suffer consequences
Isaiah 58:3

6. If employer dishonest, employees become dishonest
Proverbs 29:12

7. Special treatment for employees who are believers
Exodus 21:2
Deuteronomy 15:12-14

» Employer blessed for having godly employees
Genesis 30:27
Genesis 39:5

8. Faithful employer
Nehemiah 5:14-18

9. Unfaithful employer
Exodus 1:13-14

10. Be selective in hiring employees
Proverbs 26:10

b. Employees responsibilities

1. Be faithful
Daniel 6:4

» Serve godly employer even more faithfully
1 Timothy 6:2

» Success can be result of employee faithfulness
Proverbs 17:2
Proverbs 27:18
Daniel 6:28

c. Example of employees so faithful that accountability not required

2 Kings 12:15
2 Kings 22:7

» Example of supervised faithful employees
2 Chronicles 34:12

» Faithful employee a blessing to employer
Proverbs 25:13

2. **Be obedient to employer because actually serving Lord**
Ephesians 6:5-8
Colossians 3:22-24
Titus 2:9-10

» **Even when working for unreasonable employer**
1 Peter 2:18-19

3. **Honour your employer**
1 Timothy 6:1
Titus 2:9

4. **Do not slander your fellow employees**
Proverbs 30:10

5. **Be content with your wage**
Luke 3:14

6. **Act with moral integrity**
Genesis 39:7-9

iv. General principles of work and business

a. **Do not be in business partnership with unbelievers**
2 Corinthians 6:14-17

b. **Build business before building house**
Proverbs 24:27

c. **Productivity creates certain amount of clutter**
Proverbs 14:4

d. **Skilled people will be honoured**
Proverbs 22:29

e. **Do not presume upon tomorrow in business**
James 4:13-15

f. **Attend to your own business working with your hands**
1 Thessalonians 4:11-12

g. **Ungodly people will sometimes persecute the godly to protect a wicked business**
Acts 19:24-28

h. **The Lord can use work to humble us**
Psalm 107:11-12

i. **Fair remuneration required for goods and services**
1 Kings 5:6
2 Chronicles 2:9-10

1. **Example of unfair remuneration**
1 Kings 9:10-12

j. **Retirement**
Number 8:24-26

k. **The excellent wife works hard and is a blessing to her household**
Proverbs 31:10-28
Titus 2:4-5

1. **Empty pursuits result in poverty**
Proverbs 12:11
Proverbs 28:19

SAVING AND INVESTING

i. Is saving/investing scripturally legitimate?

a. Verses that seem to legislate against saving

Matthew 6:19-21
Matthew 6:24-33
Matthew 19:16-21
Mark 6:8
Luke 5:11
Luke 12:22-34
Luke 18:18-30

1. We can save and invest only if we also give
Luke 12:13-21

b. Parable using saving and investing

Matthew 25:14-28
Luke 19:12-24

ii. Investment goals

a. Acceptable investment goals

1. Providing for your family
1 Timothy 5:8

2. Leaving an inheritance

» It is proper to leave an inheritance
Proverbs 13:22
Proverbs 19:14
Isaiah 38:1
2 Corinthians 12:14

» Old Testament laws of inheritance
Leviticus 25:46
Numbers 27:8-11
Numbers 36:2-9
Deuteronomy 18:8
Deuteronomy 21:15-17
Ezekiel 46:16-18

» The Lord and the tithe were the Levites' inheritance
Numbers 18:20-24
Ezekiel 44:28-30

» Examples of leaving an inheritance
Genesis 15:2-4
Genesis 24:35-36
Genesis 25:5
Genesis 31:14-16
Genesis 48:21-22
Joshua 24:32
Ruth 4:5-10
2 Chronicles 21:3
Ecclesiastes 5:13-14
Ecclesiastes 7:11

» A blessing of godly obedience was the ability to leave and receive an inheritance
1 Chronicles 28:8
Ezra 9:12
Psalm 25:12-13
Proverbs 17:2

» Parable using inheritance as an illustration
Luke 15:11-31

» Jesus responds to inheritance question
Luke 12:13-15

» Inheritance given too soon will not be a blessing
Proverbs 20:21

» It was practice to appoint a guardian until heir was old enough to manage the estate
Galatians 4:1-2

» It is vain to work hard to leave inheritance to the unwise or having no heirs
Ecclesiastes 2:18-21
Ecclesiastes 4:8

b. Unacceptable investment goals

1. The desire to become rich
1 Timothy 6:9

» When we desire to become rich we are loving money
1 Timothy 6:10

» Flee the temptation to become rich
1 Timothy 6:11

SAVING AND INVESTING CONTINUED

» **Worship only the Lord**
Matthew 4:8-10
Luke 4:5-8

iii. Saving
Proverbs 21:20
Proverbs 30:24-25

a. **Example of saving for a future need**
Genesis 41:34-36

iv. God's framework for successful investing

a. **Know where the Lord wants you to invest**
Isaiah 48:17

b. **Diversify**
Ecclesiastes 11:2

1. **Business/vocation before acquiring home**
Proverbs 24:27

» **Those who owned homes**
Matthew 8:14
Mark 1:29
Luke 4:38

» **Those who did not own a home**
Matthew 8:20
Acts 28:30

c. **Avoid risky investments**
Ecclesiastes 5:13-14,16

d. **Be a steady plodder**
Proverbs 21:5

1. **Do not be hasty**
Proverbs 21:5
Proverbs 28:20
Proverbs 28:22

e. **Timing important**
Ecclesiastes 3:1

f. **Seek counsel**
(See *Counsel section*)

g. **Know financial condition to provide for needs and accomplish objectives**
Proverbs 27:23-27
Luke 14:28-29

h. **Planning and order encouraged**
Proverbs 20:18
Proverbs 21:5
Proverbs 24:3-4
1 Corinthians 14:40
1 Corinthians 14:33

v. Instructions to successful investors

a. **Do not be proud**
Jeremiah 9:23-24
1 Timothy 6:17
James 1:9-11

b. **Do not trust in riches**
Jeremiah 48:7
Jeremiah 49:4-5
1 Timothy 6:17

c. **Give generously**
1 Timothy 6:18

d. **Do not become inaccessible**
Isaiah 5:8

2,350 VERSES ON MONEY

i. General investing principles

a. Pay a fair price for an investment

Leviticus 25:14-17

1. Some deceive to avoid paying fair price
Proverbs 20:14

ii. Acceptable for a wife to invest

Proverbs 31:10, 16, 24

iii. Lending

a. Old Testament believer was to lend to needy believers

Deuteronomy 15:7-9

1. The lender was blessed
Psalm 112:5

2. New Testament extended obligation to those who asked for loan
Matthew 5:42

b. No interest was to be charged

Exodus 22:25
Leviticus 25:35-37
Deuteronomy 23:19

1. Example of violating this law
Nehemiah 5:3-12

2. Blessed if interest not charged
Deuteronomy 23:20
Psalm 15:1, 5
Ezekiel 18:7-17

3. Cursed if interest charged
Proverbs 28:8
Ezekiel 18:10, 13
Ezekiel 22:12-13
Habakkuk 2:6-7

4. Permissible to charge a foreigner interest
Deuteronomy 23:20

c. A necessity was not to be taken to secure a loan

Exodus 22:26-27
Deuteronomy 24:6, 10-13
Deuteronomy 24:17

1. Accusation of violating this law
Job 22:5-6

2. Blessed if no such pledge taken
Ezekiel 18:7, 9, 16-17
Ezekiel 33:15

3. Cursed if such a pledge taken
Ezekiel 18:10, 12-13
Amos 2:6, 8

» Wicked take such pledges
Job 24:3, 9

d. Loan repayment was not required

1. Debts forgiven every seven years
(See *Debt section*)

2. In New Testament, lend even to enemies expecting no return
Luke 6:34-35

CHILDREN

i. Parents are responsible for teaching their children godly principles and practices of life

Deuteronomy 4:9
Deuteronomy 6:6-7
Deuteronomy 11:18-19
Proverbs 22:6

BUDGETING

i. Know your financial condition

a. To be able to provide for needs

Proverbs 27:23-27

b. To be able to successfully accomplish objectives

Luke 14:28-29

ii. Our lives should exhibit order

1 Corinthians 14:40

a. Lord is not a God of confusion

1 Corinthians 14:33

iii. Planning encouraged

Proverbs 20:18
Proverbs 21:5
Proverbs 24:3-4

CONTENTMENT   COVETING

i. Contentment is learned/enabled by the Lord

Philippians 4:11-13

» Be content/not anxious because Lord is our provider
Matthew 6:25-34
Luke 12:22-31
Hebrews 13:5-6

» Be content with basic needs of life satisfied
1 Timothy 6:8

» Be content with your salary
Luke 3:14

» Contentment comes largely because of a desire for Christ
Psalm 73:25

ii. Contentment and godliness yield great gain

1 Timothy 6:6

iii. A husband of an adulteress will not be content

Proverbs 6:35

i. Commanded not to covet

Exodus 20:17
Deuteronomy 5:21
Deuteronomy 7:25

a. Punishment threatened for coveting

Joshua 6:18
Micah 2:1-3

1. Example of punishment for coveting
Joshua 7:11-25

2. Examples of coveting given to instruct us
1 Corinthians 10:6

b. The covetous shall not inherit the Kingdom of God

1 Corinthians 6:9-10

1. Covetous person is an idolater
Ephesians 5:3, 5

c. Do not associate with a covetous believer

1 Corinthians 5:9-11

d. Example of godly person not coveting

Acts 20:33

ii. God can control coveting

Exodus 34:23-24

iii. Coveting used as illustration of the function of the law

Romans 7:7-8

EVIL USES OF MONEY

i. Betrayal of Jesus

Matthew 26:14-15
Matthew 27:3-10
Mark 14:10-11
Luke 22:3-5
Acts 1:18

ii. Brothers sold into slavery

Genesis 37:28

iii. Money paid for divination

Numbers 22:7
Numbers 22:18
Numbers 24:13

iv. Money offered for attempted murder of Jewish race

Esther 3:9-11
Esther 4:7

v. Money paid to harm Samson

Judges 16:4-5
Judges 16:18

vi. Money paid for murder

Judges 9:4

GREED

i. Commanded not to be greedy

Ephesians 5:3, 5

a. Greed is idolatry

Colossians 3:5

b. Guard against every form of greed

Luke 12:15
1. Exercise self-control if you tend to be greedy
Proverbs 23:1-3

c. When Christ becomes our desire, greed not a problem

Psalm 73:25

d. Example of godly person who was not greedy

1 Thessalonians 2:5

ii. The Lord punishes greed

a. As an example to His children

1 Corinthians 10:6
1. What the greedy desired
Numbers 11:4-5

b. Example of greedy people

1 Samuel 14:32
1. Greedy leaders
Isaiah 56:11
2. Greedy people are wicked
Romans 1:28-29
Psalm 10:3-4
3. Greed will capture the greedy
Proverbs 11:6

4. False prophets will exploit the body of Christ out of greed
2 Peter 2:1-3
2 Peter 2:14-15

5. There are those who will never be satisfied
Proverbs 30:15

6. Religious people can be greedy
Ezekiel 33:31

c. Example of Lord punishing greedy people

Numbers 11:34
2 Kings 5:20-27
Jeremiah 6:12-13
Jeremiah 8:10

IDOLATRY

i. Commanded not to be an idol worshipper
Exodus 20:23

a. Idols are the work of people's hands
Psalm 115:4
Psalm 135:15

1. God provides everything, even material used for idols
Hosea 1:8, 13

b. Greed equated with idolatry
Colossians 3:5

ii. God judges those who worship idols
Ezekiel 23:29-30
Micah 1:7

» Example of God's people destroying idols, then Lord blessing
Isaiah 30:22-23

iii. Example of idolatry cloaked in religion
Judges 17:2-4

PARTIALITY

i. Lord is not partial
Deuteronomy 10:17
2 Chronicles 19:7
Job 34:19
Ephesians 6:9

ii. We are not to be partial
Proverbs 28:21

a. It is sin to be partial
James 2:8-9

b. Do not be partial to the rich
James 2:1-9

c. Do not be partial to the poor
Exodus 23:3
Leviticus 19:15

d. Leaders/judges are not to be partial
Deuteronomy 1:17
Deuteronomy 16:18-19
2 Chronicles 19:6-7

iii. Cursed if partial
Malachi 2:9

iv. Correct attitudes

1. Be of the same mind towards one another
Romans 12:16

a. Consider others more important than yourself
Philippians 2:3

TAXES/TRIBUTE

i. Commanded to pay taxes

Romans 13:5-7

a. Jesus approved of paying taxes

Matthew 22:17-21
Mark 12:14-17
Luke 20:22-25

ii. Examples of taxes paid

2 Kings 3:4
2 Kings 15:20
2 Kings 23:33, 35
Ezra 6:8

a. Special reward – taxes not required to be paid

1 Samuel 17:25

b. No taxes/tribute required of Levites

Ezra 7:24

c. Jesus paid temple tax to avoid offence

Matthew 17:24-27

iii. Examples of tribute paid

1 Kings 4:21
2 Kings 17:1-3
2 Chronicles 17:5
2 Chronicles 17:12
2 Chronicles 27:5
2 Chronicles 36:3
Ezra 4:20

a. Threat of tribute not paid

Ezra 4:13

POOR

i. Commanded not to oppress the poor

Exodus 22:21-24
Job 34:28
Proverbs 28:3

a. Wicked oppress the poor

Isaiah 32:6-7

1. Description of people oppressing the poor

Proverbs 28:15
Proverbs 30:14

b. Judgement on those who oppress the poor

Job 20:10, 15, 18-20, 26, 28
Psalm 37:14-15
Psalm 109:11, 16
Proverbs 22:16
Proverbs 22:22-23
Isaiah 3:14-15
Isaiah 10:1-2
Jeremiah 22:1-5
Ezekiel 22:7, 29
Amos 2:6-7
Amos 4:1-2
Amos 5:9-12
Amos 8:4-6
Zechariah 7:9-12
Malachi 3:5

1. Request for the Lord to judge oppression of the poor

Psalm 94:2, 6, 7

c. Example of oppressing the poor

Jeremiah 2:34

1. Religious people oppressing the poor

Mark 12:38-40
Luke 20:46-47

d. Oppressing the poor is common

Ecclesiastes 5:8

ii. Defend/help the poor/helpless

Proverbs 31:8-9
Isaiah 1:17
Jeremiah 21:12

a. Godly people help the poor

Proverbs 29:7
Job 30:25

b. Lord blesses those who help the poor

Psalm 41:1-3
Proverbs 19:17

1. Blesses leader who helped the poor

Proverbs 29:14
Jeremiah 7:5-9

2. Feed the poor and the Lord will repay

Luke 14:12-23

c. Judge the poor fairly

Exodus 23:6
Deuteronomy 24:17

d. Show mercy to the poor

Daniel 4:25-27

e. Those who do not defend the poor will be judged

Jeremiah 5:27-29

1. Sin of Sodom, not helping the poor

Ezekiel 16:49

2. Example of leader who did not defend poor

Isaiah 1:23

f. How we treat the poor reflects upon the Lord

Proverbs 14:31
Proverbs 17:5

iii. God's part with the poor

a. Lord provides for/protects the poor and needy

Deuteronomy 10:18
Job 5:15
Psalm 9:18
Psalm 10:14
Psalm 12:5
Psalm 34:6
Psalm 35:10
Psalm 40:17
Psalm 68:6
Psalm 68:10
Psalm 69:33
Psalm 102:17
Psalm 107:4
Psalm 109:31
Psalm 113:7
Psalm 132:15
Psalm 140:12
Psalm 146:7
Psalm 146:9
Psalm 147:6
Proverbs 15:25
Isaiah 11:4
Isaiah 14:30
Isaiah 25:4
Isaiah 41:17
Jeremiah 20:13

1. **Prayer for Lord to help the poor**
Psalm 72:4, 10, 12-15
Psalm 74:21
Psalm 82:3-4
Psalm 109:21-22

2. **Humanity's view of God's part and the poor**
Job 24:2-12, 14

b. God's perspective of the poor

Revelation 2:9
Revelation 3:17-18

1. **Lord chose weak to shame the strong**
1 Corinthians 1:26-27

2. **Lord made all people**
Proverbs 22:2
Proverbs 29:13

3. **Humanity's perspective of poor**
Ecclesiastes 6:8

iv. Problems and benefits for poor

a. Problems for the poor

1. **Poor have few friends**
Proverbs 14:20
Proverbs 19:4
Proverbs 19:7

2. **Poor suffer injustice**
Proverbs 13:23

3. **Poor relate to rich meekly**
Proverbs 18:23

4. **Poor serve rich**
Proverbs 22:7

5. **Poor are ignored**
Ecclesiastes 9:14-16

6. **Poverty**
Proverbs 10:15

7. **Prayer not to be poor**
Proverbs 30:7-9

b. Benefits for poor

1. **Poor are called blessed**
Luke 6:20, 24

2. **Poor are rich in faith**
James 2:5

3. **Gospel is preached to the poor**
Isaiah 61:1
Matthew 11:2-5
Luke 4:18
Luke 7:22

4. **Poor will not be kidnapped for riches**
Proverbs 13:8

5. **Poor who know the Lord will be comforted in heaven**
Luke 16:19-25

6. **Poor can glory as children of God**
James 1:9-10

7. **During restoration of Israel, poor will benefit**
Isaiah 29:19

8. **Poor, but wise, understand the rich**
Proverbs 28:11

9. **Things poverty better than**
Proverbs 19:1
Proverbs 19:22
Proverbs 28:6

v. Examples of poor

1 Samuel 18:23
Psalm 70:5
Psalm 86:1
Lamentations 1:11
Luke 2:22-24
1 Corinthians 4:11-12
2 Corinthians 6:4-5, 10

2 Corinthians 11:27
Philippians 4:11-14

a. Poor/rich in church

1 Corinthians 11:18-22

vi. Giving to the poor

a. Return of land

Leviticus 25:11-13

b. Laws regarding poor becoming slaves

Leviticus 25:39-54

1. **Not obeying laws resulted in judgement**
Jeremiah 34:13-17

vii. Miscellaneous

a. Things that make a person poor

Proverbs 13:18
Proverbs 20:13
Proverbs 21:17
Proverbs 23:20-21

b. No poor in land if people fully obeyed

Deuteronomy 15:4-5

c. Only poor left in defeated land

2 Kings 24:14
2 Kings 25:12
Jeremiah 39:10
Jeremiah 40:7
Jeremiah 52:15

» **Other areas addressing poor:
Lending, Partiality, Work**

RICHES

i. Biblical perspective of possessions

a. Lord's perspective of riches

Revelation 2:9

1. People's perspective of possessions
Job 5:5
Job 15:29
Job 20:10, 15, 18-20, 26, 28
Job 21:13, 16
Job 22:23-25
Job 27:13, 16-17
Job 36:11
Job 36:19
Ecclesiastes 7:11-12

b. We take nothing with us when we die

Psalm 49:16-20
Ecclesiastes 5:13-15
1 Timothy 6:7
Psalm 39:6

c. You cannot buy redemption for your soul

Psalm 49:5-8
Proverbs 11:4
Matthew 16:26
Mark 8:36-37
Luke 9:25

d. Riches produce many "friends"

Proverbs 14:20
Proverbs 19:4

e. Wealth is fleeting

Proverbs 23:4-5
Hebrews 11:24-26
1 Peter 1:7
1 Peter 1:18

f. All possessions are nothing compared to knowing Jesus

Philippians 3:7-8

g. Riches are uncertain

1 Timothy 6:17

1. Riches useless apart from the Lord
Ecclesiastes 2:4-11

h. Things more valuable than riches

Job 28:15-19
Psalm 37:16
Psalm 119:14
Psalm 119:72
Psalm 119:127
Proverbs 3:13-16
Proverbs 8:10-11
Proverbs 8:18-21
Proverbs 15:16
Proverbs 16:8
Proverbs 16:16
Proverbs 16:19
Proverbs 19:1
Proverbs 20:15
Proverbs 22:1
Proverbs 28:6

i. Much required from those who have been given much

Luke 12:48

ii. Blessings of wealth

a. Righteous will be rewarded with prosperity

Proverbs 13:21
Proverbs 15:6

b. Wealth for person who meditates on Word of God

Psalm 1:1-3

c. The prosperous will worship the Lord

Psalm 22:29

RICHES CONTINUED

d. Praying for prosperity

Psalm 106:5
Psalm 122:6-7
Psalm 128:5
3 John 2

1. Rich godly people

Genesis 12:5
Genesis 13:2
Genesis 15:13-14
Genesis 24:1
Genesis 24:16
Genesis 24:35
Genesis 26:12-14
Genesis 30:43
Genesis 33:11
Genesis 41:42
Genesis 45:13
Genesis 46:6
Genesis 47:27
Joshua 22:8
Ruth 2:1
2 Samuel 1:24
1 Kings 10:4, 7
1 Kings 3:11-13
1 Chronicles 29:23
1 Chronicles 29:28
2 Chronicles 1:11-12
2 Chronicles 9:22
2 Chronicles 17:5
2 Chronicles 17:11-12
2 Chronicles 18:1
2 Chronicles 32:27-30
Nehemiah 9:25
Job 1:3
Daniel 3:30
Matthew 27:57
1 Corinthians 4:8, 11-12
Philippians 4:11-18

e. Lord delights in prosperity of His servants

Psalm 35:27

f. Not all will prosper

Hebrews 11:36-40

g. Jesus is worthy to receive riches

Revelation 5:12

h. The wise can become rich

Proverbs 14:24

i. How wealth is acquired

Proverbs 24:3-4

1. Things that keep people from wealth

Proverbs 21:17
Proverbs 22:16

iii. Dangers of wealth

a. Loving wealth

Psalm 62:10

b. Pride

Ezekiel 28:4-5
1 Timothy 6:17

1. Rich should not be proud because life is short

James 1:9-11

2. Boast in Lord not riches

Jeremiah 9:23-24

c. Riches afford a sense of security

Proverbs 10:15
Proverbs 18:11
Psalm 30:6-7

1. Those who trust in riches

Psalm 49:10-12

d. Wealth tends to separate people

Genesis 13:5-11
Genesis 26:12-16
Genesis 36:6-7
Isaiah 5:8

1. Riches can separate Christians

1 Corinthians 11:18-22

e. **Riches are deceitful/can choke fruitfulness**

Proverbs 11:18
Matthew 13:4-5, 7, 22
Mark 4:2-3, 7, 18-19
Luke 8:7, 14

f. **Hard for rich to enter Kingdom**

Matthew 19:16-26
Mark 10:17-27
Luke 18:28-30

1. **Rich who do not know Lord will be separated from Him for eternity**
Luke 16:19-25

g. **Rich think they are wise**

Proverbs 28:11

h. **How the rich treat the poor**

Proverbs 18:23
Proverbs 22:7
James 2:6-7

i. **Wealth can contribute to forgetting the Lord**

Deuteronomy 6:10-12
Deuteronomy 8:9-18
Deuteronomy 31:20
Proverbs 30:7-9
Jeremiah 22:21-22
Revelation 3:17-18

j. **Wealth creates envy**

Genesis 26:12-14, 16
Genesis 31:1

iv. Curses of wealth

a. **Curse of kidnapping**

Proverbs 13:8

b. **Curse of lack of sleep**

Ecclesiastes 5:12

c. **Woes pronounced upon the rich**

Luke 6:24
James 5:1-5

v. Why do the wicked prosper?

Psalm 10:3-5
Psalm 37:1-2, 7, 9-11
Psalm 73:1-20
Proverbs 11:16
Jeremiah 12:1-2

a. **Ungodly rich**

1 Samuel 25:2
Esther 1:4
Esther 5:11
Isaiah 2:7
Ezekiel 27:33
Daniel 11:2
Luke 19:2

b. **Commanded not to seek prosperity of particular people**

Deuteronomy 23:6
Ezra 9:12

vi. Wrong way to prosper

a. **Some prosper by sinning without acknowledging sin**

Hosea 12:8
Zechariah 11:5

» **Some act religious to prosper**
Judges 17:13

vii. Miscellaneous

Proverbs 2:4
Ecclesiastes 10:20

RICHES CONTINUED

a. **People sometimes deceive as to their financial status**

Proverbs 13:7

b. **Money used to illustrate the value of the Kingdom of God**

Matthew 13:44-46

c. **Righteous living equated with silver**

Proverbs 10:20

d. **Judgement on wealthy, ungodly nations**

Isaiah 15:7
Jeremiah 51:13
Ezekiel 27:3, 12-27
Hosea 10:1-2
Zephaniah 1:11, 13, 18
Zechariah 9:3-4

e. **The king was not to become too rich**

Deuteronomy 17:16-17

1. **Kings disobeyed command not to become too rich**
1 Kings 4:26
1 Kings 10:14-28
2 Chronicles 1:14-17
2 Chronicles 9:8-27

f. **Prophecy**

Psalm 45:12
Isaiah 39:2, 4-6
Isaiah 60:5-6, 9, 11
Isaiah 61:6-7
Haggai 2:7
Zechariah 1:17
Zechariah 7:7
Revelation 6:15-16
Revelation 13:16-17
Revelation 17:4
Revelation 18:3
Revelation 18:11-19

g. **Prospects of wealth used as motivation**

Genesis 34:10-12
Genesis 34:21, 23
1 Samuel 17:25

MISCELLANEOUS

a. Business

1 Kings 10:29
Proverbs 20:14
James 4:13-15

b. Financial consequences of adultery

Proverbs 5:10
Proverbs 6:35
Proverbs 29:3

c. Human heart

Proverbs 23:6-8
Ezekiel 33:31
James 3:14-16
James 4:2-3
2 Peter 2:3

d. Old Testament law concerning marriage

Deuteronomy 21:14

e. Some have no concern with money

Isaiah 13:17
2 Samuel 21:4

f. Miscellaneous

Ruth 3:10
Proverbs 11:26
Proverbs 12:9
Proverbs 23:23
Isaiah 53:9
Matthew 13:52
Mark 5:25-26
Acts 22:28

g. Do not fine the righteous

Proverbs 17:26

h. Lord's judgement

Isaiah 7:23
Isaiah 23:18

i. The Messiah will prosper

Isaiah 52:13
Isaiah 53:10

j. A relationship with the Lord cannot be bought

Isaiah 55:1-2

k. Unfaithfulness equated with harlotry

Ezekiel 16:33-34

l. Laws concerning the priests and the land

Ezekiel 48:14

m. Lord valued little by ungodly

Zechariah 11:12-13

n. More given to one who has; all taken from one who has not

Mark 4:24-25

o. Money used to illustrate angelic joy of salvation

Luke 15:8-10

p. View of ownership in the early church

Acts 2:44-45
Acts 4:32-37

q. People coming to know Lord give up costly evil things

Acts 19:18-19

r. Vindication

Genesis 20:16

s. Spoils, plunder

Genesis 34:27-29
1 Samuel 17:53

1 Kings 20:1-6, 8
2 Kings 14:12, 14
2 Chronicles 20:25
Ezra 9:7
Esther 8:11
Esther 9:5, 10
Isaiah 10:5-6
Isaiah 10:12-14
Ezekiel 26:12
Ezekiel 30:4
Hosea 13:15
Amos 3:11
Obadiah 1:13
Obadiah 1:6, 11
Micah 4:13
Nahum 2:9-10
Nahum 3:1
Habakkuk 2:6-8
Zephaniah 1:11, 13, 18
Zephaniah 2:9

t. **Lifestyle**

2 Corinthians 8:13-15
1 Timothy 2:9

u. **Restitution**

Exodus 21:18-19
Exodus 21:22
Exodus 21:28-30
Exodus 21:32-36

v. **Leaders**

1 Samuel 8:10-11, 14-17
Ezekiel 45:7-8 ,

w. **Prophecy**

Jeremiah 32:6-7, 9, 14-15
Jeremiah 32:25
Ezekiel 7:11-13, 19
Ezekiel 38:10-13
Daniel 11:24
Daniel 11:38
Daniel 11:43
Zechariah 14:1-2
Zechariah 14:14
Luke 17:28

2 Timothy 3:1-2
Revelation 6:6
Revelation 6:15-16
Revelation 9:20-21
Revelation 13:16-17
Revelation 17:4
Revelation 18:3
Revelation 18:11-19

x. **Dishonest people in church/ religious settings**

Jeremiah 7:5-9, 11
Micah 3:11
Matthew 21:12-13
Mark 11:15-17
Luke 19:45-46
John 2:14-16
2 Corinthians 12:14
1 Timothy 3:2-3
1 Timothy 3:8
1 Timothy 6:5-6
Titus 1:10-11
1 Peter 5:1-2

y. **Perspective**

1. **One who loves money will never get enough**
Ecclesiastes 5:10-11

2. **Miscellaneous verses**
Song of Solomon 8:7
Isaiah 24:2
Isaiah 52:3
Lamentations 4:1-2
Matthew 22:5
Luke 12:13-15
Luke 16:1-14
Acts 8:18-24
1 Corinthians 10:33
2 Corinthians 6:4, 10
Colossians 3:1-5
1 Timothy 4:4
Hebrews 10:34
Hebrews 11:24-26
1 John 2:15-17

3. **Good in spite of money offered for evil**
2 Samuel 18:11-12

4. **Mercenary**
   1 Kings 15:16-20
   2 Kings 16:5, 8-9
   2 Chronicles 16:2-4

5. **Litigation**
   Isaiah 59:2, 4
   Matthew 5:25-26
   Matthew 5:40
   Luke 6:29-30
   Luke 12:58-59
   1 Corinthians 6:1-8

6. **The wicked oppose the work of God when it costs them money**
   Acts 16:16-19
   Acts 19:24-27

NOTES

NOTES

NOTES

NOTES

NOTES

NOTES